W9-BLC-480

Bicycling in Florida

The Cyclist's Road and Off-Road Guide

Second Edition

TOM OSWALD

Pineapple Press, Inc.
Sarasota, Florida

*To Sheila. I could never have
done this without your help. Thank you!*

Inquiries should be addressed to:

Pineapple Press, Inc.
P.O. Box 3889
Sarasota, Florida 34230

www.pineapplepress.com

Library of Congress Cataloging-in-Publication Data

Oswald, Tom.
  Bicycling in Florida : the cyclist's road and off-road guide / Tom Oswald.-- 2nd ed.
    p. cm.
  ISBN-13: 978-1-56164-403-2 (pbk. : alk. paper)
  1. Cycling--Florida--Guidebooks. 2. All terrain cycling--Florida--Guidebooks. 3. Florida--Guidebooks. I. Title.
  GV1045.5.F6O78 2007
  796.6'409759--dc22
                        2007030304

Second Edition
10 9 8 7 6 5 4 3 2 1

Printed in the United States of America

ACKNOWLEDGEMENTS

Thanks to all of the bike shop employees and owners, club members, and other Florida cyclists who graciously contributed their time, expertise, and advice. This is your book.

Thanks to the staff at Pineapple Press for all their hard work in making the updates for this second edition.

And thanks to Amanda Oswald for your help and advice and for first suggesting this was something I could do. Otherwise, it would never have occurred to me.

In case you did not yet know, cycling is an inherently dangerous activity. You can get hurt or even killed riding a bicycle. Do so at your own risk. You must use your own judgment to determine if your skill, experience, and level of conditioning are appropriate for the situations and conditions you might encounter. The only person that can assume responsibility for your decisions and actions is you; neither the author nor the publisher will assume responsibility for accidents or injuries that occur while engaging in activities outlined in this book. It's your life. Live it.

TABLE OF CONTENTS

NORTHEAST
Overview 42

ROAD RIDES 43

OFF-ROAD RIDES 62

CENTRAL WEST
Overview 86

ROAD RIDES 87

OFF-ROAD RIDES 99

Introduction

So you want to ride your bike in Florida. Well, you could not have picked a nicer place. Blessed with some of the nicest weather to be found on planet Earth, plus gorgeous scenery and moderate terrain that is perfect for self-propelled conveyance, the Sunshine State is indeed a cyclist's paradise. And the purpose of this book is to help you find and enjoy some of its many wonders. Herein lies valuable information, instructions, maps, and advice, designed to be useful to all manner of riders, from complete novices to lifelong cyclists, from skinny-wheeled road riders to knobby-tired mountain bikers.

So top off your water bottles, pump up your tires, and grab your helmet. Let's saddle up and ride.

HOW TO USE THIS BOOK

This first section contains a general introduction to cycling in the state of Florida, its weather, its terrain, the conditions you can expect to encounter on its roads and trails, and a brief summary of its traffic laws regarding bicycles. Also included are some suggestions on the clothing and equipment you will need to make your cycling experiences as fun, safe, comfortable, and satisfying as possible.

The following sections are each dedicated to a specific geographic region of the state. Following a brief introduction and overview of the region, each section contains directions, descriptions, and maps (see the map legend at the end of the introduction) for some of the best rides in the area. These rides have all been tried, tested, and carefully mapped out. Every effort has been made to choose routes that will be safe and enjoyable for the majority of riders. However, please be sure to read the descriptions and compare them with an honest evaluation of your own skill, confidence, and fitness level before setting out, in order to avoid getting into something beyond your expectations or capabilities. The rides are divided into two categories: road and off-road. Road rides are considered to be any cycling that occurs on a paved surface. This includes not only the regular highways and byways, but also paved rail-trails and other bike paths. The road rides are doable on just about any type of bike, but those with narrower, high-pressure tires are generally better suited. You can use a mountain bike or other fat-tired cruiser, but on these the scenery goes by just a little too slowly for most people's taste. If you do much pavement riding, you will be best served by a road racing, touring, or hybrid bike.

The off-road rides are almost exclusively the domain of the fat-tired bike. And the multi-speed variety, as opposed to the one-speed beach cruiser, is the best choice for this type of riding. There are a few of the off-road rides that are on firm enough ground that they could be tackled on a hybrid or cyclocross bike, but for the most part the Florida soil is too sandy to support the narrower tires. They just sink in and bog down too easily.

There are a few things about the rides that require further explanation. First of all, some of the abbreviations used in road names. The interstate abbreviation (for example, 1-75) is quite obvious, but here are a few more that you will encounter:

Abbreviation	What it Stands For	Example
US	national highway	US 301
SR	state road	SR 50
CR	county road	CR 1024
FR	forest road	FR 4

On some of the rides there are optional directions for either extending or shortening the outing. These optional directions are enclosed in parentheses. You are encouraged, of course, to use these rides as a jumping-off place for your own explorations, but be advised that the maps included here may not be detailed enough to guide you in far-ranging diversions from the printed routes. For some that will be just fine, but those adventurers who like the comfort of having a good map along may want to carry a local road map or USGS topographical map of the area.

Also included in each section is a list of other places in the region where you can ride your bike. These lists include some road rides, but since roads are relatively easy to find—they are all over the place in Florida—the lists mainly focus on places to ride off-road, which are usually harder to come by. Not all of these "other" rides have been mapped out, but there are directions telling you how to get there and sources to contact for additional information.

A listing of contact information for some of the region's cycling clubs and organizations is also included at the end of each section. Such groups are usually full of friendly, fun-loving cycling enthusiasts. They are a valuable resource for information about other riding available in the area, ride times and meeting places for group rides, races, rallies, festivals, and all sorts of other two-wheeled fun.

THE LAWS

Those who are interested in all the legal mumbo jumbo can get the specifics from the Department of Transportation, but here are the rules regarding bicycles boiled down to the basics. Following these guidelines and using some courtesy and common sense should keep you out of too much trouble.

- All bicyclists under the age of 16 are required to wear a helmet.
- When operating on a roadway, bicyclists have the same rights and obligations as motorists. Obey all traffic signals. When turning, signal your intent to turn for at least 100 feet before the turn.
- When riding on a sidewalk (which may not be allowed by some local governments), bicyclists have all of the same rights and obligations as pedestrians. Bicyclists must yield to pedestrians and give an audible signal when passing.
- Keep at least one hand on the handlebars at all times when you are in motion.
- When traffic is moving faster than you, stay as far to the right-hand edge of the roadway as practicable. You can leave the right-hand edge when making a left turn, when passing, to avoid road hazards, or when the lane you are in is too narrow to be safely shared by a bicycle and a car at the same time.
- When turning left you are entitled to the full use of the lane from which the turn is made.
- Cyclists may ride two abreast—but no more than two abreast—

and only if doing so will not impede the flow of traffic.

- Do not wear any headset or headphones other than a hearing aid while riding.
- Bicycles are not permitted on restricted access roadways such as interstate highways.
- Local governments of towns, cities, and counties may have other laws and ordinances regarding bicycle use. Contact local law enforcement agencies for specifics.

THE WEATHER

Although newcomers to the state are often heard to complain about a lack of seasons, any native can tell you that there are actually two very distinct seasons in Florida: hurricane season and tourist season. But seriously, there really are seasons. The differences between them are perhaps a bit more subtle than most people are used to, but the seasons are there nonetheless.

Winter is the season for which Florida is most famous, and for good reason. Throughout December, January, and February Florida routinely enjoys some of the warmest temperatures in the country. But it is a big state, and things can vary quite a bit from one end to the other. In the northern portions of the state, the average lows are usually in the 40s, with an occasional plunge below freezing. Every once in a while there is even a light dusting of snow. Average winter highs are in the 60s. The south Florida average lows are only in the 50s, with highs in the 70s. It is this kind of balmy weather that attracts visitors and retirees in droves and also makes for pleasant year-round cycling.

Summers in Florida are definitely hot, but surprisingly, the summer highs, which are often around 90, are no hotter than it gets in much of the rest of the country. But the heat does start occurring earlier in the year and lingers longer. The good news is that things almost always cool down at least into the 70s overnight, which makes for excellent riding conditions in the early mornings.

Summer is Florida's rainy season, and it is not uncommon for some places to experience up to 10 inches of rain in a month. Most of this precipitation comes from the often short, but very intense, thunderstorms that regularly sweep the peninsula on sultry summer afternoons. These storms are often welcome relief, as they cool things down dramatically in their passing. The rest of the year is not nearly as wet; most other months receive only 2 to 3 inches of rain. Annual rainfall averages throughout the state range from around 45 to 65 inches per year.

Spring and fall are perhaps the least conspicuous of Florida seasons and also the most ideal for cycling. The temperatures are usually moderate and comfortable. You can ride just about whatever time of day you want. There is little rain and therefore little concern about getting caught in it. And in spring, especially in north and central Florida, you also get to experience Florida at its most florid, when there are colorful blooms on practically every vine, shrub, tree, and bush.

THE TERRAIN

Much of the terrain in Florida, especially in the coastal areas and on the entire southern tip of the peninsula, is a lot like an armadillo in the middle of I-95—dead flat. But farther inland, in central and north Florida, things can vary from gently rolling to downright hilly. Flatlanders visiting these regions will find plenty of challenge in the hills and will presently come to learn just why their bicycles came equipped with those small chainrings. Those coming from more mountainous places may not find it as challenging as their own home turf, but will be pleasantly surprised to discover that not all of Florida is as flat as it is sometimes reputed.

Of note to off-road riders, the other thing that Florida has a reputation for is sandy soil, and for the most part this is true. There is no denying the place is sandy, but it is possible to deal with.

First, choose good trails, like the ones in this book. Second, run big, wide tires at lower air pressures. And third, fourth, and fifth, have a good attitude, a fair bit of perseverance, and good technique. When you see a patch of sand coming up, try to accelerate and run at it with a good head of steam. The faster you go, the more likely you will be able to float across the top and not sink in too deeply. Pedal very smoothly at high rpms to avoid breaking the rear wheel loose. Keep your weight low and distributed evenly between both wheels, with perhaps just a tad more over the rear than the front. Avoid having too much weight on the front wheel or making any sharp turns. Either mistake can cause the front wheel to furrow in and stop abruptly, pitching you over the handlebars if you are going fast.

HAZARDS

Riding in Florida is probably not any more dangerous than riding anywhere else, but some of the hazards might be a bit different from those in other places. All riders should be aware of the dangers posed by the intense rays of the Florida sun. Dehydration, heat exhaustion, and heat stroke are all possible results of riding under-prepared or at the wrong time of day. And sunburn, besides being uncomfortable, can lead to irreversible skin damage and even skin cancer. All of these maladies can be prevented by taking the proper precautions, such as dressing appropriately, using sunscreen, drinking plenty of fluids, and not riding during the heat of midday.

Another danger that is more prevalent in Florida than in most other places is lightning. All areas of the state are subject to frequent thunderstorms, especially in the summer months. Of course, it is best to avoid them if at all possible, but they do sometimes come up rather quickly and can catch you unaware. If you are caught in a thunderstorm, seek shelter immediately. Buildings, automobiles, bridges, and overpasses are some of the better refuges. Underneath a tree is usually not a good place to be. They are likely lightning targets, and even if they are not struck, the high winds common in thunderstorms can cause things like coconuts, heavy limbs, and fronds to drop on you. Most of all, you want to avoid being the tallest thing, or being anywhere near the tallest thing, in the area.

Roadies will want to use extra caution in the winter months, when Florida's roads are flowing, and sometimes overflowing, with out-of-state visitors. Tourists, often not exactly sure where they are going, are known to make sudden stops and turns in the most unpredictable manner and inappropriate places. Just remember: They are usually more worried about not missing the turn for Jungle Wonders Watery Funworld than they are about turning the hapless cyclist into a human hood ornament. Florida, like every other state, has plenty of other yahoos who, drunk or sober, can give the cyclist a hard time out on the road. The best way to avoid confrontation with them, and you do want to avoid confrontation, is to either ignore them, or if you must respond, do so with the goofiest five-fingered wave you can muster. Suppress the urge to fly the old single-digit salute. That only eggs them on.

And speaking of creeps, off-road riders should be forewarned about some of the little nasties they might encounter out on the trails. Florida has more than its fair share of mosquitoes and ticks, which can carry unpleasant and even deadly diseases. They can usually be warded off by using repellent and avoiding areas where they are known to be heavily concentrated. There are also several kinds of poisonous snakes found in Florida. Contact with them can usually be avoided by giving all snakes a wide berth. Florida also has plenty of alligators, and while they pose no threat to the average trail rider, some of the rides in this book do include places to stop and swim. And if it's a body of water, and it's in Florida, there are probably alligators in it. Use your best judgment and swim at your own risk.

WHAT TO WEAR

First and foremost—whatever the weather, however long or short the ride, and wherever it is—wear your helmet. You and your loved ones will never be sorry that you did wear a helmet, only that you did not.

Throughout most of the year shorts and short-sleeved shirts or jerseys are the standard attire of the Florida cyclist. And since most of the rides in this book last at least an hour, cycling-specific shorts are highly recommended. They can be either the baggy or tight fitting kind, depending on your sense of style and level of modesty, but you (and your bottom) will be much more comfortable in something with some padding and made with the mechanics of cycling in mind.

It is also a good idea, no matter what the season, to bring along a portable windbreaker or rain jacket. The weather can change very quickly in Florida, and those sudden, unexpected showers can have a real chilling effect. A jacket, even if it doesn't keep you bone dry, will help keep you warm. Rain pants might also be desired in the cooler months, but they are usually too hot to be of use in the average summer rainstorm.

In the winter months, when morning temperatures are often in the 40s and 50s, but afternoons are in the 70s, you can hardly get by without a set of both arm and leg warmers. They are small and light to carry, easy to don and remove, and can change any pair of shorts and short-sleeved jersey into tights and a long-sleeved jersey. Arm and leg warmers, a light pair of full-fingered gloves, and an ear-warmer headband are usually sufficient for all but the chilliest days. If you plan to do a lot of cold weather riding, especially in northern Florida, then a good pair of tights and a warm long-sleeved jersey would also be nice things to have.

WHAT TO BRING

At the very top of the list is water or some other kind of drink, and plenty of it. Dehydration is one of the surest ways to turn a sweet ride sour, and Florida is one of the easiest places to dehydrate. It is also fairly easy to prevent, however, by bringing lots of water and drinking often—at least two bottles per hour if it's hot out. And for any ride longer than an hour, food is important, too. Bring something that you have eaten before and that is agreeable to your system. It is usually best to eat a little bit at a time, say every half-hour or so, rather than a big gob all at once.

You will need a good, strong, water- and sweat-proof sunscreen, especially in the summertime. And sunglasses do a lot to help reduce eyestrain in the bright Florida sun. Off-roaders and roadies who make frequent stops may want to bring along some insect repellent. The mosquitoes, ticks, biting flies, and no-see-ums can get pretty bad out in the woods and on the roadsides at times. Be careful when using repellents that contain DEET though. That stuff can destroy things that are made out of nylon, like tents, bags, packs, jackets, jerseys, cycling shorts, shoes, and socks.

And finally, those who travel far out into the boonies should consider bringing a simple first-aid kit. Things like bandages and gauze pads have their obvious uses. Adhesive tape can sometimes be used to make temporary repairs on bicycles, as well as human beings. And besides being useful for treating minor cuts and scrapes, those alcohol wipes that come in the little foil packets are also handy for cleaning your hands after completing a trail or roadside repair.

Now that you are well taken care of, it's time to think about your bike. At the bare minimum you need a spare innertube, a patch kit, tire levers, a pump, enough change to make a telephone call, and something to carry it all in. An even better kit will also include both a small Phillips and flathead screwdriver, a set of metric Allen keys (the 4, 5, and 6 mm sizes will fit most of the important bolts on most modern bicycles), a small adjustable wrench, a spoke wrench, a chain tool, and enough money to buy something to eat and drink. This may sound like an unwieldy amount of stuff to carry, but there are several nifty little multi-tool gadgets on the market today that combine all of these tools and more into one small, portable package. And most importantly, simply bringing all of these things along is not enough to get you out of a jam. You have to know how to actually use them, too. The subject is much too broad to cover here, but there are several good books on bike repair available these days, and any good bike shop should be able and willing to teach you the very basics, like innertube changing and repair.

Now you have been briefed, cautioned, dressed, hydrated, fed, equipped, and prepped. Sounds like you're ready to ride. Be careful out there, and don't forget to have fun.

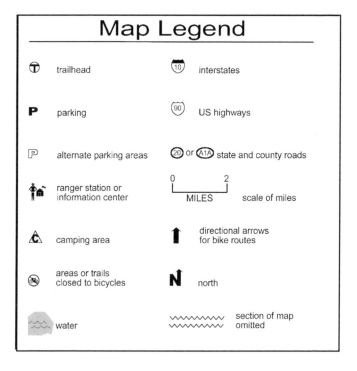

Northwest

Northwest Florida, as far as most cyclists are concerned, is the most diverse region of the state. While it has large cities like Pensacola; the popular spring break destination of Panama City; and Tallahassee, the state capital, these are greatly outnumbered by the rural areas and small towns like Ebro, Two Egg, and Havana (pronounced "Hey Vanna"). Roadies and off-roaders alike will be glad to know that the Northwest has the greatest acreage of state and national forest land in Florida, which can make for many miles of peaceful pedaling.

Northwest Florida is home to the highest point in the state, as well as several hundred miles of coastline, so it comes as no surprise that there also is great geographical variety here. The rolling hills of the northern portions provide a great workout for road riders. Mountain bikers will find the traction on the trails in these same clay hills to be exceptional. Things flatten out and get sandier nearer the coast. Those with an aversion to hills will find this to be a boon, but some off-roaders may worry that the sand will be too much of a challenge. Fear not, though. All the off-road routes in this book have been carefully chosen to avoid the most miserable sandy spots and to provide the most pleasurable rides possible.

Climatically, the summers are just about as hot and humid in northwest Florida as they are in the southern reaches of the state, with average high temperatures in the 80s and 90s. The winters are much cooler, though. In fact, northwest Florida is the only region that has any regular measurable snowfall, though its annual average is a scant 0.1 inch. Dips in temperature below the freezing point are not uncommon in January and February, but they are usually short-lived, as daytime temperatures almost always warm up into at least the 40s or 50s. Temperature swings of 30 and 40 degrees from morning to afternoon are not uncommon, making removable arm and leg warmers a must for riding in the cooler months. As for precipitation, the northwest receives more inches of rain than south Florida but has more clear days than rainy ones. Cyclists will do well to remember that when it rains, it pours in northwest Florida. They will be more comfortable and much happier if they plan their rides and dress accordingly.

So, just as in the rest of the state, cycling is definitely a year-round activity in northwest Florida. The most hospitable seasons are fall and spring, with spring offering the best scenery. Particularly in March and April, cyclists will be dazzled by the bountiful blooms of azalea, dogwood, and wild wisteria on just about any route they choose.

Plenty of recreational and competitive riding events take place year-round all over the region. The highest concentrations of cyclists and cycling events are in the larger metropolitan areas, but cyclists frequently like to head out into the more rural parts to take advantage of the quieter roads and more open spaces.

ROAD RIDES

SANTA ROSA ISLAND OUT-AND-BACK

Location: Pensacola
Distance: 21 to 35 miles
Terrain: flat and straight
Description: This ride gives you the choice of either going west into Fort Pickens for a 21-mile ride or east to Navarre Beach for a 35-miler along a beautiful stretch of coastal highway. The direction and speed of the wind should help to determine which one you choose. If the wind is strong, as it often is here, it is best to head out into the wind so that you can enjoy a nice tailwind on the way back. There are points in the road, however, that sustained damage from various hurricanes, and you may have to push through a bit of sand.

Fort Pickens, and much of the road leading up to it, is part of the Gulf Islands National Seashore. There is an entry fee for cyclists, and it is well worth it. The fort itself is quite interesting to visit, and the beaches are among the most gorgeous Florida has to offer. Those heading east to Navarre Beach will have 6 or 7 miles of business and residential districts to cross before reaching the haven of the next section of National Seashore. The beaches here are every bit as nice, and there is no entry fee.

Fees: toll to get onto Santa Rosa Island is $1 and entry to Fort Pickens is free.

Facilities: There are rest rooms and water at the beach access parking lot where the ride starts. There are also various food and convenience stores along both routes.

Finding the ride: From Pensacola, take US 98 south to Gulf Breeze, crossing the Pensacola Bay Bridge. In Gulf Breeze, 1.7 miles past the Bay Bridge, turn right onto SR 399 and cross the Santa Rosa Sound. There is a tollbooth at the end of this second bridge. Go straight at the traffic light 0.9 mile past the tollbooth and enter the beach parking lot. Both of the rides start from here.

Mileage log
West to Fort Pickens

0.0	Turn left out of the beach parking lot onto Ft. Pickens Rd.
2.5	There are rest rooms and water at the parking area on your left, the last little bit of civilization for a few miles.
3.2	Pass the Ft. Pickens entry station.
10.2	Here is the fort. Pretty cool, isn't it?
10.7	This is the end of the line. The body of water in front of you is Pensacola Bay. On the other side of the bay is Pensacola Naval Air Station. There are some rest rooms off to your right if you need them. When you are done here, turn around and go back the way you came.
14.0	There are several nice places along here to stop and enjoy the beach on your right.
18.3	You are leaving Gulf Islands National Seashore.
21.4	Turn right into the beach parking area and you are done.

East to Navarre Beach

0.0	Turn right out of the beach parking lot onto Via De Luna.
0.7	The road narrows from four lanes to two.
3.5	The traffic will continue to thin out now as you go farther

east. There are some beach access points on your right.

6.9   Enter Gulf Islands National Seashore. From here on the road may be sandy in spots.

14.3   You are now leaving Gulf Islands National Seashore.

16.8   There is a convenience store on your left.

17.7   Turn right into the parking lot at the Navarre Beach Fishing Pier. This is your turnaround point. When you are ready, turn left out of here and head back the way you came.

21.1   Enter Gulf Islands National Seashore.

28.5   Leave Gulf Islands National Seashore.

34.7   Use caution here where the road widens to four lanes and the traffic can be heavy.

35.4   Turn left into the beach parking lot, and you are done.

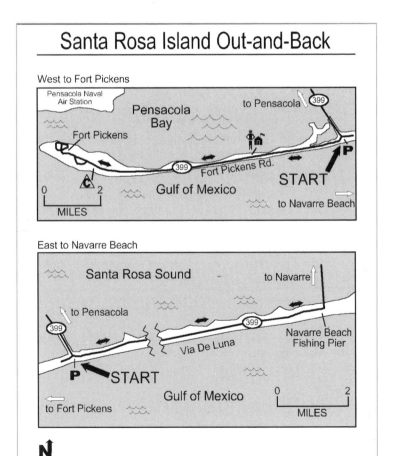

Santa Rosa Island Out-and-Back

For more information, contact:
Gulf Islands National Seashore
1801 Gulf Breeze Parkway
Gulf Breeze, FL 32563
(850) 934-2600
Website: http://www.nps.gov/guis

BLACKWATER HERITAGE STATE TRAIL

Location: Milton, 20 miles northeast of Pensacola
Distance: 16 miles
Terrain: mostly flat
Description: The Blackwater Heritage State Trail is a recent addition to Florida's ever-growing collection of rails-to-trails. Its asphalt surface spans the 8 miles between the town of Milton and the U.S. Navy's Whiting Field. As with most other rail trails, this one offers easy cycling on level surfaces, ideally suited for casual rides and family outings. On weekends, riders should plan on encountering many other trail users, including walkers, runners, skaters, and equestrians. Riders are also cautioned to ride with care in town, where there are several potentially hazardous cross streets. Plans have begun to extend the trail around Whiting Field and back down to Clear Creek, adding another 6-8 miles of trail.

Fees: none

Facilities: There are rest rooms and water available at the trailhead in Milton as well as a volunteer-operated concession on Alabama St.

Finding the ride: From I-10's exit 22, take SR 281 (Avalon Blvd.) north for 5 miles. Turn right onto US 90 for 1 mile, then turn right onto Old Hwy 90 for .7 mile. Turn right onto Tar Plant Rd., and park on the left.

Mileage log

0.0   From the southernmost trailhead located on Tar Plant Rd., head north on the paved trail.

1.0   There is another parking lot here, with restrooms and water. You will find a bike shop here at the corner of Elva St. and Stewart St.

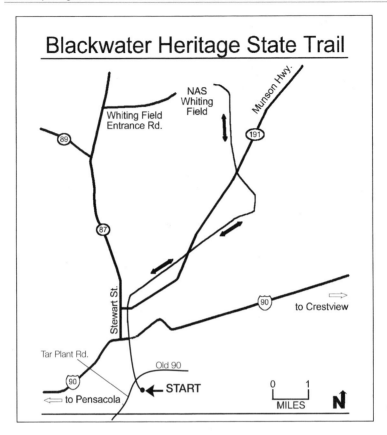

Blackwater Heritage State Trail

1.9 Pass the public library on your left. There is another parking lot here, with a welcome center and trail concessionaire. Coming soon will be a playground and public use area.

3.7 There is a parking lot for equestrians on your right. Use caution crossing SR 191 (Munson Hwy.).

4.5 Cross the long bridge over Clear Creek.

6.75 Use caution crossing over SR 191 (Munson Hwy.) again.

8.0 Where the asphalt narrows the Military Heritage Trail begins. You can either continue for an extra 1.5 miles to the east gate of Whiting Field and turn around for a 19-mile trip, or turn around at this point to complete the 16-mile round-trip.

For more information, contact:
Blackwater Heritage State Trail
5533 Alabama St.
Milton, FL 32564

(850) 983-5338
Website: www. FloridaGreenwaysandTrails.com

THE HIGHEST POINT IN FLORIDA

Location: Lakewood, Walton County
Distance: 30 miles
Terrain: moderately hilly
Description: While it is really not much to brag about, you can
still have the personal satisfaction of riding your bike up to the top
of Britton Hill, the highest point in Florida. This 30-mile loop leaves
from Lakewood Park, site of the Sunshine State's highest point at an
altitude of 345 feet above sea level, in tiny Lakewood, Florida. The
route offers little shade, so the best time to try this one may not be in
the middle of a summer afternoon. Use your own judgment. The roads
are nice—mostly smooth (although there are a few miles where this
route nips into Alabama that are a bit rough) and little traveled. There
are quite a few hills, but none are extremely long or steep. Some of the
vistas along the way make the climbs quite rewarding.

Fees: none

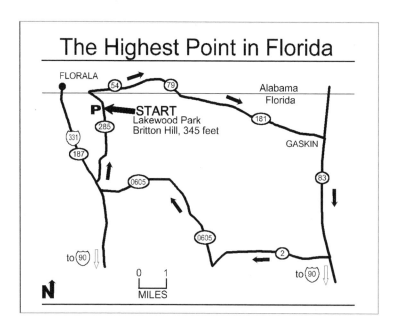

Facilities: There are rest rooms and water at Lakewood Park. Food and a telephone can be found a couple of miles north in Florala, Alabama. Camping is available at nearby Florala State Park.

Finding the ride: From I-10's exit 70 take SR 285 north for about 24 miles. Lakewood Park will be on your left, at the top of a hill, about 2.8 miles north of the point where SR 285 turns right off of US 331.

Mileage log

0.0	Turn left out of Lakewood Park onto SR 285.
0.7	Cross the state line and enter Alabama.
0.8	Turn right at the stop sign onto Alabama SR 54.
3.5	Turn right onto Covington County Route 4.
4.1	Turn right onto Covington County Route 79.
5.3	Cross the state line back into Florida. The road you are on is now called SR 181.
6.6	Cross a small bridge.
8.3	Cross another small bridge.
10.9	Enter the community of Gaskin.
11.1	Turn right at the stop sign onto SR 83.
15.5	Turn right onto SR 2 at the flashing yellow light.
20.5	Turn right onto CR 0605.
27.3	Turn right at the stop sign onto US 331/SR 285.
27.5	Turn right, staying on SR 285.
29.5	You are now beginning the final climb up to the highest point in Florida.
30.3	Turn left into Lakewood Park, and you are done.

BRUCE CAFÉ ROAD RIDE

Location: Bruce, 20 miles northwest of Panama City
Distance: 44 miles
Terrain: quite hilly
Description: The Bruce Café is a favorite place for Panama City cyclists to begin and end a ride. It is well worth the drive to get out into the country and away from city traffic, plus you can get a great pre-ride jolt of java and a well-deserved stack of flapjacks when you get back. The first and last 13 miles of the ride are on SR 81, which is wide, not

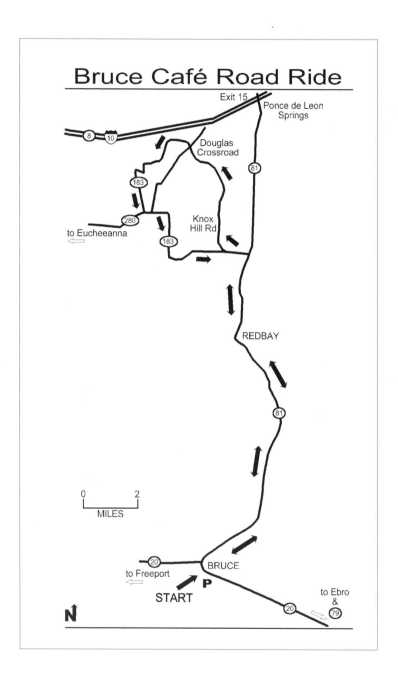

Bruce Café Road Ride

very shady, and a bit boring. But there is a good shoulder most of the way. The remainder of the ride is a loop on quiet country roads with plenty of shade and good scenery.

Fees: none

Facilities: They are serving up good grub at the Bruce Café; please do not impose upon the nice folks there for use of their rest rooms or parking lot unless you plan to stay for a bite. There are also toilets and water at Douglass Crossroads Park, near the halfway point of the ride.

Finding the ride: From Panama City, take US 98 west to Panama City Beach and then turn right onto SR 79 (north) for about 15 miles. At Ebro, turn left onto SR 20 and go west 5 miles to Bruce. The Bruce Café is on your right, at the corner of SR 20 and SR 81. Check with the folks at the café for the best place to leave your car, or just park in the empty lot across the street.

Mileage log

0.0	From the Bruce Café, turn right and go north on SR 81.
5.9	Cross a small bridge.
10.0	Pass through Redbay.
12.8	Cross the bridge over Bruce Creek.
13.5	Turn left at the yellow flashing light onto CR 183.
14.4	Turn right onto Knox Hill Rd. Knox Hill is a good, stiff climb.
19.8	Douglass Crossroads Park is on your left. There are toilets, water, and picnic tables here. Also, somewhere along here the name of the road changes to Douglass Cross Rd.
22.0	Turn left at the stop sign onto CR 183.
24.9	Turn left at the stop sign, still on CR 183.
27.9	Cross a bridge.
29.6	Pass by Knox Hill Rd., on your left.
30.5	Turn right at the red flashing light onto SR 81.
34.0	Go back through Redbay.
44.0.	You are back in Bruce and have earned yourself a pile of pancakes.

For more information, contact:
Panama City Flyers
P.O. Box 15966
Panama City, FL 32406-5966
Contact: Henry Lawrence
(850) 258-1276

THE COVE RIDE

Location: Panama City
Distance: 16 miles
Terrain: slightly hilly
Description: This ride starts and ends at the charming Oaks on the Bay Park in Panama City. The route closely follows the northern shore of St. Andrew Bay, mostly on pleasant, shady neighborhood streets. You will find plenty of good scenery, nice homes, and friendly people in this area.

Fees: none

Facilities: There is a bakery and cafe on Beck Ave., less than a block away from the park. There is also a convenience store just a bit farther, and several enticing eateries nearby.

Finding the ride: From US 98 in Panama City, take Beck Ave. south about 0.6 mile. Turn left onto 10th St., then take an immediate right into the small parking lot at Oaks on the Bay Park. If the parking lot is full, there is plenty of on-street parking in the vicinity.

Mileage log

0.0	From the parking lot at Oaks on the Bay Park, turn right onto 10th St. and then go immediately right onto Chestnut Ave.
0.1	Turn left onto 9th St.
0.6	Turn right at the stop sign onto Frankford Ave.
0.7	Turn left at the yellow flashing light onto Beach Dr.
3.0	Cross a small drawbridge.
3.4	Turn left onto Cherry St. at the end of Beach Dr.
3.7	Turn right onto Bunkers Cove Rd.
4.8	Bear right at the fork, staying on Bunkers Cove Rd.
5.0	Bear right again, still on Bunkers Cove Rd.
5.3	Turn right at the stop sign onto Hollis Ave.
5.4	As you go around this left curve, Hollis Ave. becomes Bonita Ct.
5.5	Turn right onto Bonita Ave.
5.9	Turn right onto Harris Ave.
6.0	Turn right at the stop sign onto DeWitt St.
6.1	Turn right at the four-way stop sign onto Cove Terrace Dr.
6.6	Turn left at the stop sign onto Cove Ln.

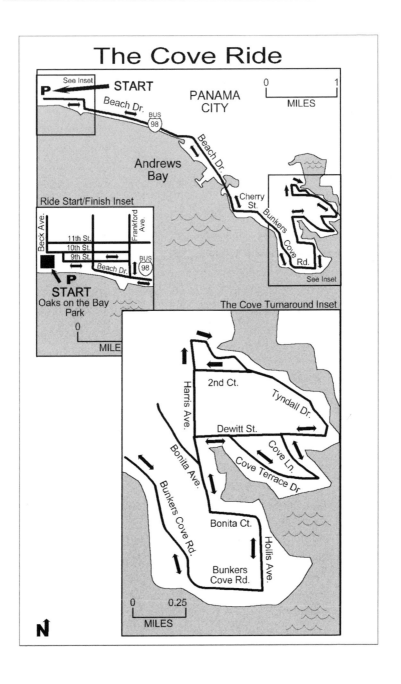

The Cove Ride

6.8	Turn right at the four-way stop sign onto DeWitt St.
7.0	DeWitt St. becomes Tyndall Dr.
7.5	Turn left onto 2nd Ct., at the baseball field.
7.7	Turn right at the four-way stop sign onto Harris Ave.
7.9	Turn right at the stop sign onto 3rd St. and then immediately turn right onto Tyndall Dr. When you get to the baseball field, you will be heading back the way you came.
8.6	Tyndall Dr. becomes DeWitt St.
8.9	Turn left onto Cove Ln. at the four-way stop sign.
9.1	Turn right onto Cove Terrace Dr.
9.6	Turn left onto Dewitt St. at the four-way stop.
9.8	Turn left onto Harris Ave.
9.9	Turn left onto Bonita Ave. at the stop sign.
10.1	Turn left onto Bonita Ct.
10.3	Turn right onto Hollis Ave.
10.5	Turn left onto Bunkers Cove Rd.
10.7	Turn left at the stop sign, staying on Bunkers Cove Rd.
10.9	Turn left at the stop sign, still on Bunkers Cove Rd.
12.0	Turn left onto Cherry St.
12.4	Turn right onto Beach Dr. at the yellow flashing light.
15.0	Turn right onto Frankford Ave.
15.1	Turn left onto 9th St.
15.6	Turn right onto Chestnut Ave.
15.7	Turn left onto 10th St., and then turn left into the parking lot at the park.

For more information, contact:
Panama City Flyers
P.O. Box 15966
Panama City, FL 32406-5966
Contact: Henry Lawrence
(850) 258-1276

TALLAHASSEE-ST. MARKS HISTORIC RAILROAD STATE TRAIL

Location: Tallahassee
Distance: up to 32 miles

Terrain: flat

Description: The Tallahassee-St. Marks Historic Railroad State Trail is a paved recreational trail that occupies the former railroad corridor spanning the 16 miles between the capital city and the fishing village and Gulf port of St. Marks. The trail is open to cyclists, skaters, joggers, and walkers, with a separate dirt trail for equestrians. Its out-and-back orientation and car-free environment should make this ride appealing to just about all manner of riders, from families with young children to grizzled, veteran road warriors. You cannot get lost as long as you stay on the paved trail. Simply ride out as far as you like, then turn around and go back. Those who go the whole distance to St. Marks will want to visit the fort at the San Marcos de Apalache State Historic Site or treat themselves to a cold beer and some fresh oysters or other piscatorial delights at Riverside Cafe, a local favorite. Just remember

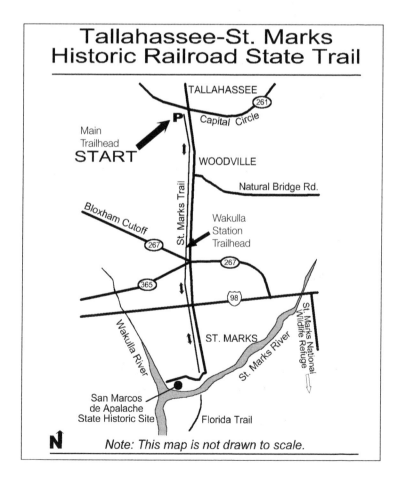

Tallahassee-St. Marks Historic Railroad State Trail

Note: This map is not drawn to scale.

that you still have 16 miles to go. Woeful has been many the rider who overindulged at this halfway haven.

Fees: none

Facilities: Water, rest rooms, snacks, and bike-washing facilities are offered at the main trailhead. There are benches at intervals along the trail. Riverside Cafe and a small market are in St. Marks.

Finding the ride: From Tallahassee, take Monroe St. south. Just past the Leon County Fairgrounds, 2.3 miles south of the Capital building, the road will turn into Woodville Hwy. Continue south for about 2 more miles. The trailhead parking is on your right, 0.2 mile past the junction with Capital Circle Southeast (US 319).

Mileage log

0.0	Head south on the paved trail.
1.3	On your right is the Munson Hills trailhead. There is a rest room and water available here.
2.5	Lewis Hall Park is another water and rest room stop.
3.9	Use caution going through Woodville. The people are plenty friendly, but there are lots of cross streets to negotiate.
8.9	Here is the Wakulla Station trailhead, which has rest rooms, a picnic shelter, and a playground.
9.8	Use caution crossing Bloxham Cutoff and SR 365.
12.9	Use caution crossing US 98.
16.0	This is the end of the trail. Welcome to St. Marks. A right turn will take you to the fort and a beautiful view of the river. A left will take you to Riverside Cafe and a small store with drinks and snacks. Just hop back on the trail and head north when you are through here.
19.3	Use caution crossing US 98.
22.4	Use caution crossing Bloxham Cutoff and SR 365.
27.3	Watch for cross traffic while going back through Woodville.
31.2	You are back at the main trailhead.

For more information, contact:
Florida Department of Environmental Protection
Office of Greenways and Trails
3900 Commonwealth Blvd MS 795
Tallahassee, FL 32399-3000
(850) 245-2052
Website: www.FloridaGreenwaysandTrails.com

WACISSA SPRINGS VIA OLD ST. AUGUSTINE RD.

Location: Tallahassee
Distance: 43
Terrain: hilly in places
Description: Old St. Augustine Rd. is one of the canopy roads that have made the Tallahassee area so popular with road cyclists. These shady, tree-covered routes radiate outward from the center of town like spokes from a wheel hub. The canopies, being comprised mainly of Spanish moss-draped live oaks, stay green all year long but are at their fullest in the warmer months, just when their shade is most needed.

This out-and-back ride departs from Myers Park, near downtown Tallahassee, and visits Wacissa Springs, a great place for a rest, a

One of the canopy roads of Tallahassee

picnic, and a refreshing swim in the cool, clear waters. Riders may encounter some heavy traffic in the first few miles, which will thin out as they get farther into the countryside. The first and last 10 miles, on Old St. Augustine Rd. and Williams Rd., are shady, curvy, and fairly hilly. The middle 20 miles, on Tram Rd., are flat, straight, and mostly shadeless, but relatively free of cars. Be sure to wear sunscreen and bring plenty of water if you plan to do this one in the summer.

Fees: none

Facilities: Rest rooms, water, and a telephone are available at Myers Park. There are no facilities, other than the woods, the spring, and some picnic tables, at Wacissa Springs.

Finding the ride: From the intersection of Monroe St. (US 27) and Tennessee St. (US 90), take Monroe St. south for 0.6 mile. Turn left onto

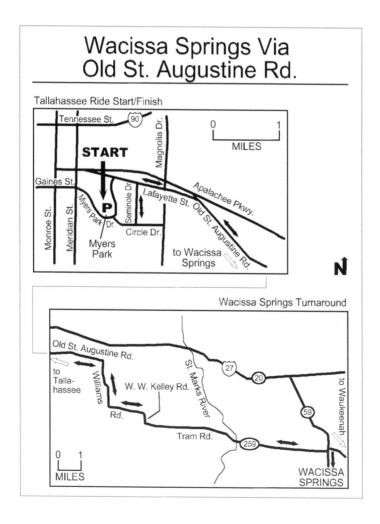

Caines St., which changes to Myers Park Dr. after 0.3 mile. Continue for another 0.3 mile and turn left into the parking lot near the baseball diamond at Myers Park.

Mileage log

0.0	Turn left onto Myers Park Dr. from the parking lot near the baseball diamond.
0.2	Turn right onto Circle Dr.
0.5	Turn left at the four-way stop sign onto Seminole Dr.
0.9	Turn right at the traffic light onto Lafayette St.
1.2	Go straight at the traffic light at Magnolia Dr.
1.6	The road changes names here, from Lafayette St. to Old St. Augustine Rd.
3.5	Cross Capital Circle SE.
7.8	Turn right at the stop sign onto Williams Rd.
1.7	Turn right at the stop sign onto W. W. Kelley Rd.
12.0	Turn left at the stop sign onto Tram Rd.
15.0	Enter Jefferson County.
16.1	Cross the St. Marks River.
20.3	Turn right at the stop sign onto SR 59 in Wacissa. (If you go straight instead, it is 5 miles to Waukeenah, where there is a convenience store with cold drinks.)
21.6	You are at the entrance to the parking lot at Wacissa Springs There are picnic tables and a place to swim here. When you are done, head back north on the road you came in on.
22.9	Turn left onto Tram Rd.
27.1	Cross back over the St. Marks River.
28.2	Enter Leon County.
31.2	Turn right onto W. W. Kelley Rd.
31.5	Turn left onto Williams Rd.
35.4	Turn left onto Old St. Augustine Rd.
37.6	You are now climbing the dreaded Church Hill.
39.7	Cross Capital Circle SE.
42.0	Cross Magnolia Dr.
42.1	Cabos Tacos, on your right, is a favorite post-ride place to eat.
42.3	Turn left onto Seminole Dr. at the traffic light.
42.7	Turn right at the four-way stop sign onto Circle Dr.
43.0	Turn left onto Myers Park Dr.
43.2	Turn right into the parking lot at Myers Park, and you are

done.

For more information, contact:
Capital City Cyclists
P.O. Box 4222
Tallahassee, FL 32315-4222
Hotline: (850) 847-8433
Website: www.cccyclists.org

OFF-ROAD RIDES

UNIVERSITY OF WEST FLORIDA POWER LINE TRAILS

Location: Pensacola
Distance: about 5 miles
Terrain: moderately challenging single-track
Description: This is a fun little network of trails on the University of West Florida campus. It is not extremely hilly here, but there are a few short climbs—all middle-chainring stuff. There are a couple of drop-offs that will require either expert technique or a dismount to safely negotiate. There are also some sandy stretches of trail along the way, all of which should be manageable for most riders. While offering pleasant cycling in the fall, winter, and spring, this place is known to sometimes be miserably buggy in the summertime. Come prepared with repellent and plenty of water if you want to tackle this one in the warmer months.

Fees: none

Facilities: There are rest rooms and water available at the baseball stadium, just a bit west of the trail parking area.

Finding the ride: From Davis Hwy. (Alt. US 90), just south of the Davis Hwy./Scenic Hwy. (US 90) junction, head west for 0.3 mile at the signs for the University of West Florida on Campus Blvd. Take the first left at the sign for the track and soccer field and park near the track. The trail starts in the woods nearby.

Mileage log

0.0   Enter the woods on the single-track that is on your left when you face the running track. Follow the main trail.

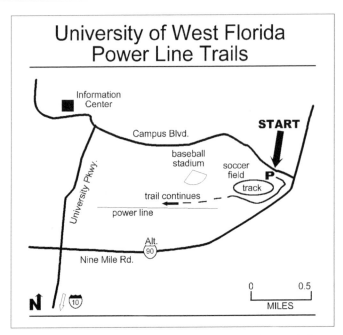

University of West Florida
Power Line Trails

Information Center

Campus Blvd.

START

baseball stadium

soccer field

P

University Pkwy.

track

trail continues

power line

Alt. 90

Nine Mile Rd.

0   0.5

MILES

N   10

0.4   You are now on the opposite side of the track from where your car is parked. Proceed west along the fenceline, toward the baseball and softball fields.

0.8   You have just passed the baseball stadium on your right. Continue along the fenceline/power lines for a couple hundred yards, then take the first single-track you see on your right. There are so many interconnecting, unmarked trails here that it is impossible to give accurate and explicit instructions for navigating them. But fear not; this is a small area, and it is virtually impossible to get lost for more than five minutes. A good rule of thumb is to take all right-hand turns until you find yourself near Campus Blvd. (the paved road). Then begin making left-hand turns until you come back out near the power lines. When you are done romping here it is a simple matter to just go back along the power lines the way you came, past the ball fields, through the woods, and back to the parking lot.

For more information, contact:
University of West Florida
University Parkway

On the campus of the University of West Florida

Pensacola, FL 32501
(850) 474-2000
Website: www.uwf.edu

BLACKWATER FIGURE EIGHT

Location: Blackwater River State Forest
Distance: 19 miles
Terrain: easy to moderate forest roads
Description: This 19-mile figure eight starts and ends at the Hurricane Lake Campground in the Blackwater River State Forest. The route offers some shade along the way and a chance to swim in the river. If you are not sure that you are adept at handling sand, this might not be the ride for you. While most of the roads are hard-packed clay, there are some sandy sections, which could prove problematic for the uninitiated. This would be a great moonlight ride, into which you could incorporate a refreshing sans-chamois dip in the Blackwater River. Be sure to bring some friends, though. It gets kind of spooky out in these woods at night. And besides, it's no fun swimming alone.

Fees: none

Facilities: There are rest rooms and water available at the campground. There are showers, too, but they are reserved for

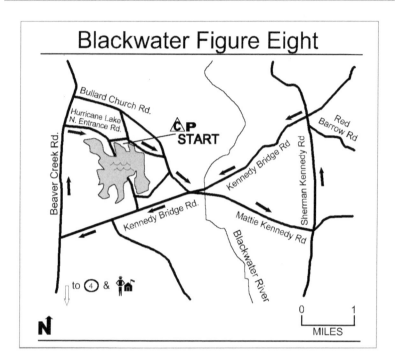

registered campers only. Cold drinks and snacks can be found at the market on the corner of CR 191 and SR 4 in Munson.

Finding the ride: From the intersection of CR 191 and SR 4 in Munson, proceed east on SR 4 for 2.8 miles. Turn left onto Hurricane Rd. for 3.8 miles. Go straight at the stop sign. Hurricane Rd. is now called Beaver Creek Rd. After 5 miles on Beaver Creek Rd., turn right at Bullard Church onto Bullard Church Rd. for 1.2 miles. Turn right onto the dirt road at the signs for the campground and boat ramp. Take the left fork after 0.4 mile, and 0.7 mile later you enter the campground. Drive around the campground loop and park near the boat ramp.

Mileage log

0.0	Leave the campground on the dirt road you came on.
0.7	Take the right branch at the fork.
1.1	Turn right at the stop sign onto Bullard Church Rd. (FR. 18).
2.5	Cross a small bridge.
3.3	Turn left at the stop sign onto Kennedy Bridge Rd. (FR 24).
3.6	Cross the Blackwater River on Kennedy Bridge. There are some steps on your right that lead down to the water if you

are ready for a swim.

3.7   Take the right branch of the fork onto Mattie Kennedy Rd. (FR 30).

4.7   You just made it up the toughest climb on this ride.

5.4   Cross a small bridge.

6.1   Turn left at the stop sign onto Sherman Kennedy Rd. (FR 57).

8.2   Turn left at the stop sign onto the paved Red Barrow Rd. (FR 2B).

8.5   Turn left at the stop sign onto Kennedy Bridge Rd. (FR 24), and you are back on the dirt again.

11.3   Cross over the Blackwater River on Kennedy Bridge again. How about that swim now?

11.6   If you have had enough you can turn right here, go back the way you came, and be back at the campground in 3.3 miles. If you want to get in a few more miles, go straight here.

14.4   That was a long, tough uphill you just finished. Your reward is a right turn at the stop sign onto the paved Beaver Creek Rd. (FR 31).

16.8   Turn right onto the dirt Hurricane Lake N. Entrance Rd. (FR 41).

17.7   Turn left at the signs for the campground and boat ramp.

18.1   Take the right branch at the fork.

18.9   You are back at Hurricane Lake Campground.

For more information, contact:
Blackwater Forestry Center
11650 Munson Highway
Milton, FL 32570
(850) 957-6140 extension 4

TIMBERLAKE TRAIL

Location: Eglin Air Force Base, Fort Walton Beach
Distance: 6 miles
Terrain: moderate single-track
Description: A recreation permit is required to use this trail,

which lies within the boundaries of Eglin Air Force Base. The permit costs around $7, is valid for up to one year, and it may be obtained by mail or in person. For more information, see the directions and address under Finding the Ride. Considering the dearth of other legal single-track in the vicinity, the excellent quality of this trail, and the fact that riders without permits are subject to a stiff fine, the Timberlake Trail is well worth the price of admission. This is a great all-around trail, with something for everyone. The terrain is sandy in stretches, and there are a couple of fairly tough climbs along the way. The single track varies from being tight and technical to open and fast. There is usually some kind of wildlife to be found on this ride, be it snakes, 'gators, 'possums, or 'coons.

Fees: Eglin Air Force Base recreation permit: $7

Facilities: There are no facilities available at Timber Lake. All manner of services can be found in Ft. Walton Beach.

Finding the ride: To obtain a recreation permit in person, you have to visit the Jackson Guard. Take SR 85 north out of Ft. Walton Beach to Niceville. Turn left at the junction of SR 85 and SR 20, staying on SR 85. Go 0.2 mile farther and turn right into the parking lot at the signs for the Jackson Guard. The office is open Monday through Saturday.

To get to the trail from the Jackson Guard office, take SR 85 south for 6.7 miles. Turn right onto SR 189 for 2.7 miles. At the small brown sign for Timberlake Pond Campsite and Roberts Pond, turn right and

Enjoy the view at Timber Lake, Eglin Air Force Base.

go west for 0.5 mile. Turn right onto the dirt road and follow it 0.8 mile down to the lake. Park off to the left when you get to the lake.

To get to the trail from Ft. Walton Beach, take Beal Pkwy./Lewis E. Turner Blvd. (SR 189) north for 3.1 miles past its intersection with Racetrack Rd. (SR 188). At the small brown sign for Timberlake Pond Campsite and Roberts Pond, turn left and go west for 0.5 mile. Turn right onto the dirt road and follow it 0.8 mile to the lake. Park off to the left when you get to the lake.

Mileage log

0.0   From where your car is parked, turn left onto the double-track that circles around the lake. Go just a few yards, then turn left onto the single-track that goes up into the woods.

0.6   There is a trail going off to the left. Ignore it and stay to the right.

1.0   Cross a ravine at the south end of the lake.

1.2   Along this section you will see some trails branching off to the right of the main trail. These dip down closer to the lake and then rejoin the main trail. They can be a little more challenging to ride. Stay to the left at each fork you see for the next 0.5 mile if you want the easier route.

1.8   You are at the north end of the lake. Go past the pavilion on your right and follow the double-track clockwise around the lake, heading back toward your car.

1.9   Turn left onto the single-track at the corner of the double-track and the road you drove in on, just before you get to your car.

3.2   Stay to the left at the fork.

3.3   The road that is off to your left is SR. 189.

3.5   Cross a dirt road.

4.2   Cross another dirt road.

4.3   Cross yet another dirt road.

5.9   Cross over the dirt road you drove in on, then go downhill on the wide track.

6.0   Turn right onto the narrow single-track.

6.1   You are back at your car.

For more information, contact:
Eglin Air Force Base Natural Resources Branch
107 Highway 85 North
Niceville, FL 32578
(850) 882-4164

DUTCH TIEMANN TRAIL

Location: Pine Log State Forest, 15 miles northwest of Panama City
Distance: 4.6 miles
Terrain: easy to moderate single-track
Description: This pleasant 4.6-mile loop starts and ends at the Environmental Center in Pine Log State Forest. Meandering through a young pine forest and along Pine Log Creek, this ride runs in conjunction with the Florida Trail (the cross-Florida hiking trail) for about a mile. Cyclists are welcome on the Dutch Tiemann Trail, which is blazed in light blue, and the small stretch that it shares in common with the Florida Trail, which is blazed in orange. The rest of the Florida

Dutch Tiemann Trail

to Ebro
&
(20)

Florida
Trail

P

(79)

0   0.5

MILES

Environmental Rd.

START

Florida Trail

Car Body Rd.

to Panama City
&
(98)

N

Pine Log Creek

Trail, however, is for hiking only. Riders will encounter just a little bit of sand and practically no hills, making this a fast, fun spin through the woods.

Fees: none

Facilities: Water, rest rooms, grills, picnic tables, swimming, and camping are available at the Environmental Center. The showers are only for campers. There is a small store in Ebro, 1.4 miles north on SR 79, at the intersection with SR 20.

Finding the ride: From Panama City, take US 98 west. Turn right onto SR 79 (north) at Panama City Beach for about 15 miles. Take the first left after crossing a bridge and entering Washington County, onto the dirt Environmental Rd. for 0.4 mile. Take the first dirt road on the right and continue past the large map board on the right. Go between the two lakes and park in the parking area on the left.

Mileage log

0.0   Starting from the large map at the entrance to the Environmental Center, follow the orange (Florida Trail) and

	blue (Dutch Tiemann Trail) blazes off to the west (your left as you stand looking at the map) around the lake.
0.3	The Florida Trail breaks off to the right. Stay to the left and follow the light-blue blazes.
0.4	The red-blazed campground trail breaks off to the left. Stay to the right.
0.6	Go diagonally across a dirt road intersection.
2.3	Cross a dirt road. A right here will take you to primitive campsite #1 and a nice view of Pine Log Creek.
2.5	There is a low-lying section of trail here. You may need to walk a bit if it is very muddy.
2.7	Cross a dirt road.
2.9	Turn left onto a dirt road. If you go straight across to primitive campsite #2, there is another nice view of the creek.
3.2	The dirt road makes a left here. Go straight into the woods at the sign for campsite #3. There is another view of the creek here.
3.7	The trail turns right here.
3.9	Cross a small, narrow bridge. Just past this bridge the Florida Trail joins in from the right. Stay left.
4.2	Cross a dirt road. This is Environmental Rd.
4.5	Go straight at this trail intersection.
4.6	You are back at the big map board.

For more information, contact:
Division of Forestry
Pine Log State Forest
5583-A Longleaf Rd.
Ebro, FL 32437
(850) 535-2888

MUNSON HILLS

Location: Apalachicola National Forest, Tallahassee
Distance: 11 miles
Terrain: easy to moderate single-track
Description: Many cyclists, including this writer, have cut their

first single-track teeth on this venerable trail. One of the oldest and still one of the finest examples of trail building and planning in the state, this well-used trail has stood the test of time. There are some sandy patches, but none too long to be ridden if you keep your speed up. The few hills are very modest grades. This trail is easy enough that the novice can ride nearly all of it, but its difficulty increases exponentially with speed (and in some places it really begs for it), so the veteran single-tracker can still find it exhilarating.

Fees: none

Facilities: Water, rest rooms, a telephone, snacks, and bike-washing facilities are offered at the trailhead. There are also in-line skate (for the paved St. Marks Trail) and bike rentals available.

Finding the Ride: The Munson Hills trail is accessed from the paves Tallahassee-St Marks Historic Railroad Trail. From Tallahassee, take Monroe St. south. Just past the Leon County Fairgrounds, about 2.3 miles south of the Capital building, stay to the left at the fork in the road and you will then be on Woodville Hwy. Continue south for about 2 more miles. The trailhead parking is on your right, 0.2 mile

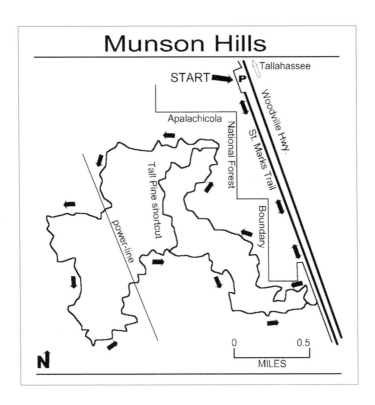

past the junction with Capital Circle Southeast (US 319).

Mileage Log

0.0	Starting from the parking lot of the St. Marks Trail, get on the paved trail and head south.
1.3	Turn right where the sign hanging over the trail points you toward the Munson Hills Trail. There are some benches and a water fountain here.
1.4	There is a map and information kiosk here and a toilet farther off to your left. Turn right where the trail splits and follow the blue blazes.
3.9	The Tall Pine Shortcut breaks off to the left here. If you go left and follow the white blazes and left again when you get to the main trail you can be back at the pavement in 2.4 miles. Stay to the right here and stick with the blue blazes to go the whole way around.
5.3	Go straight across this wide, sandy swath underneath the power lines.
7.5	Go straight and cross underneath the power lines again
7.9	You will pass the Tall Pine Shortcut, which will be on your left. Stay to the right.
9.2	You are back at the kiosk. Turn right.
9.3	Turn left onto the paved trail.
10.6	You are back at the trailhead parking lot.

For more information, contact:
USDA Forest Service
Wakulla Ranger District
57 Taff Dr.
Crawfordville, FL 32327
(850) 926-3561

LAKE JACKSON LOOP

Location: Elinor Klapp-Phipps Park, Tallahassee
Distance: 6 miles
Terrain: easy but hilly double-track
Description: Phipps Park is a great place to go and get away from

the city without having to actually leave Tallahassee. Only 5 miles away from the center of town, the 670-acre park is a boon to those Capital City inhabitants who yearn for wide open spaces. Since it is so close to town, many cyclists prefer to pedal the few short miles to the park rather than fire up the old smogmobile. Once you get there you will find about 12 miles of multi-use trails that you can share with hikers, runners, dog-walkers, and equestrians. The trails are mostly double-track forest roads with a high clay and relatively low sand content, making for a fast, firm ride on the rolling hills. There is also the Redbug Bicycle Trail, which offers 3 miles of bikes-only single-track fun.

Fees: none

Facilities: Water, rest rooms, and a telephone are available at the park. There is a convenience store 2 miles south on Meridian Rd.

Finding the ride: From central Tallahassee, take Meridian Rd. north for about 5 miles. Turn left at the MERIDIAN YOUTH SPORTS

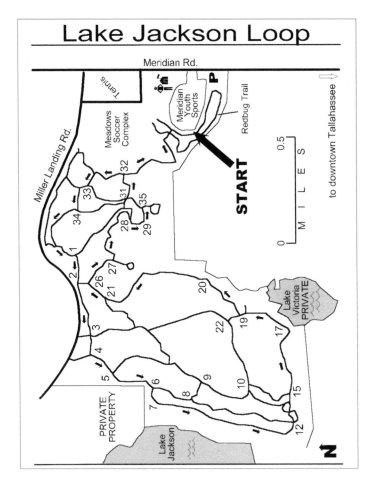

COMPLEX sign 2.5 miles after crossing the I-10 overpass. Park on the grass on the left just inside the entrance, or follow the pavement around the ballfields and park near the office. Ride the pavement clockwise around the ballfields until you come to the hiking trailhead. Twenty-five yards to the right of the hiking trailhead is a gate where the blue-blazed Redbug Trail emerges from the woods. That is where the ride begins.

Mileage log

0.0	Enter the Redbug Trail at the gate next to the hiking trailhead.
0.3	Leave the Redbug Trail and turn left onto the double-track. Turn left again when you get to the soccer fields.
0.4	Turn right, still going along the edge of the soccer fields.
0.5	Turn left into the woods on the white-blazed trail.
0.7	Cross a double-track and continue on the white-blazed trail.
1.0	Turn left at the power lines.
1.1	Continue straight where the white-blazed trail turns left.
1.5	Turn left at the gate and the equestrian trailhead. You are now on a double-track.
1.6	Turn right at marker #1.
1.7	Go straight at marker #2.
2.0	Go straight at marker #3.
2.1	Turn left at marker #4 and enjoy a nice downhill.
2.4	Turn right at marker #6.
3.1	Go straight at marker #12.
3.2	Go straight at marker #15.
3.6	Turn left at marker #17, along an old barbed-wire fence.
3.9	Turn right at marker #19.
4.7	Turn right at marker #26.
4.8	Turn left at marker #27.
5.1	Turn right at marker #28.
5.3	Turn left at marker #29, and left again at marker #35.
5.4	Turn left at marker #31.
5.5	Turn right onto the white-blazed single-track and skirt back around the soccer fields the way you came.
6.0	Turn right onto the Redbug Trail.
6.2	You are now back at the beginning.

For more information, contact:
Elinor Klapp-Phipps Park

c/o Tallahassee Parks and Recreation Department
912 Myers Park Dr.
Tallahassee, FL 32301
(850) 891-3866

LAKE OVERSTREET FIGURE EIGHT

Location: Tallahassee
Distance: 6 miles
Terrain: easy double-track
Description: The Lake Overstreet addition to Alfred B. Maclay State Gardens is a great place for casual or beginning off-road cyclists to stretch their legs. It also makes a nice warm-up or cool-down for the trails directly across the road at Elinor Klapp-Phipps Park. The toughest part of the ride described here is the short piece of single-track near the office at Phipps Park, where the ride starts. Beginners may need to walk some of this section, but will find smooth sailing the rest of the way. The wide dirt paths around Lake Overstreet are made mostly of hard-packed clay, which is very easy and enjoyable to ride on. The gorgeous Lake Overstreet is one of very few remaining examples of a truly pristine freshwater lake in the state of Florida. It is definitely worth a visit.

Fees: entry to Lake Overstreet is <$5

Facilities: Water, rest rooms, and a telephone are available at Phipps Park. There is a convenience store 2 miles south on Meridian Rd.

Finding the ride: From central Tallahassee, take Meridian Rd. north for about 5 miles. Turn left at the MERIDIAN YOUTH SPORTS COMPLEX sign 2.5 miles after crossing the I-10 overpass. Park on the grass on the left just inside the entrance, or follow the pavement clockwise around the ballfields and park near the office.

Mileage log

0.0	Starting from the office at Phipps Park, follow the signs for the bike trail to Lake Overstreet.
0.2	The tennis courts are on your left. Follow the signs across the grass parking area.
0.4	Cross Meridian Rd. and enter the Lake Overstreet addition

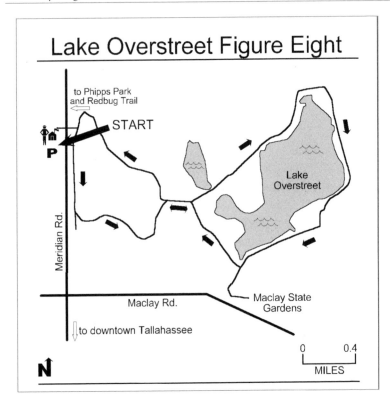

Lake Overstreet Figure Eight

to Phipps Park
and Redbug Trail

START

P

Meridian Rd.

Lake
Overstreet

Maclay Rd.

Maclay State
Gardens

to downtown Tallahassee

0   0.4

MILES

N

	of Maclay State Gardens. Don't forget to feed the honor fee box here. Have a look at the big map, then turn right onto the double-track.
0.8	Turn left.
1.3	Turn right.
1.5	Take the left branch of the fork.
2.0	There is a nice spot to view the lake off to your right. Continue straight to stay on the main trail.
4.0	Turn right here. A left will take you to Maclay State Gardens.
4.4	Turn left.
4.6	Take the right branch of the fork.
5.4	You are back at the map and the crosswalk. Cross back across Meridian Rd. and follow the signs across the grass parking area.
5.6	The tennis courts are off to your right. Enter the woods and follow the path.
5.8	You are back at the park office.

For more information, contact:
Alfred B. Maclay State Gardens
3540 Thomasville Rd.
Tallahassee, FL 32308
(850) 487-4556

REDBUG TRAIL

Location: Elinor Klapp-Phipps Park, Tallahassee
Distance: 3 miles
Terrain: moderate single-track, with a few difficult spots
Description: This short but sweet piece of single-track requires some fairly technical riding in places. It twists, turns, and undulates through some thick, jungly woods with lots of exposed roots and a couple of creek crossings. The trail is easy to find and navigate—just follow the blue blazes. Be sure not to ride on the yellow-blazed trail, which is for hikers only. Most riders like to combine the Redbug with either a lap around Lake Overstreet or a spin down to Lake Jackson and back.

Fees: none

Facilities: Water, rest rooms, and a telephone are available at the park. There is a convenience store 2 miles south on Meridian Rd.

Finding the ride: From central Tallahassee, take Meridian Rd. north for about 5 miles. Turn left at the MERIDIAN YOUTH SPORTS COMPLEX sign 2.5 miles after crossing the I-10 overpass. Park on the grass on the left just inside the entrance, or follow the pavement around the ballfields and park near the office. Ride the pavement clockwise around the ballfields a short way and you will see the trailhead, with a large map and a description of me trail on your left.

Mileage log

0.0	Enter the Redbug Trail at the trailhead and follow the blue blazes.
0.4	There is a large fallen tree that you probably need to dismount for, followed by some whoop-de-doos and a steep drop-off.
0.6	There is a wet creek crossing here.

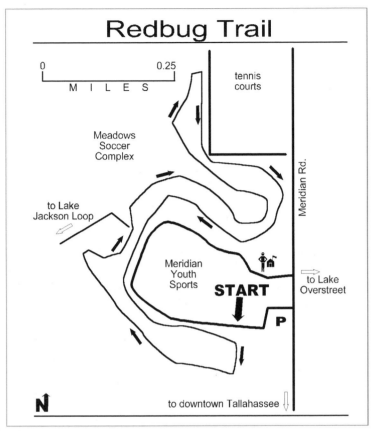

0.7	Cross the creek again, this time on a bridge.
0.8	Cross a double-track dirt road, then a small bridge with a steep, rooty climb on the other side.
0.9	Cross another bridge.
1.1	Here is another tricky little climb.
1.2	You are up near the dirt road again.
1.3	Follow the trail to the left when you get to this small clearing.
1.6	Up near the soccer fields the trail takes a sharp right turn.
2.1	You are now near the tennis courts.
2.2	Cross the service road.
2.3	You are near the park office.
2.4	Cross the service road again.
2.5	There is a nice downhill here on a wide section of trail with some berms you can jump.
3.0	You are back at the trailhead.

For more information, contact:
Elinor Klapp-Phipps Park
c/o Tallahassee Parks and Recreation Department
912 Myers Park Dr.
Tallahassee, FL 32301
(850) 891-3866

OTHER RIDES IN NORTHWEST FLORIDA

ROAD

The Seven Hills to the Sea Bike Tour is a six-day, 283-mile bike tour that links six state parks in a large loop, beginning and ending at Wakulla Springs State Park, just south of Tallahassee. Free maps and directions are available from the Florida Department of Environmental Protection.
Contact:
Florida Department of Environmental Protection
Office of Greenways and Trails
Mail Station 795
3900 Commonwealth Boulevard
Tallahassee, FL 32399-3000
(850) 487-4784

Timpoochee Trail is a scenic, 19-mile paved bike path that parallels Highway 30-A through the beaches of South Walton.
Contact:
Beaches of South Walton Visitors Center
(800) 822-6877

OFF-ROAD

The Fort Pickens Trail at Gulf Islands National Seashore offers a 6-mile, out-and-back ride on a double-track of crushed shell and sand. Located west of Pensacola Beach off of SR 399, the park charges an entrance fee.

> Contact:
> Gulf Islands National Seashore
> 1801 Gulf Breeze Parkway
> Gulf Breeze, FL 32561
> (850) 934-2600

Wakulla Springs State Park has 10 miles of graded dirt roads. The park has an entrance fee and is located 15 miles south of Tallahassee on SR 267.

> Contact:
> Edward Ball Wakulla Springs State Park
> 550 Wakulla Park Drive
> Wakulla Springs, FL 32327
> (850) 224-5950

Manatee Springs State Park has 8.5 miles of double-track loops suitable for all levels of riders. The park is located west of Chiefland on CR 320 and charges an entrance fee.

> Contact:
> Manatee Springs State Park
> 11650 NW 115th Street
> Chiefland, FL 32626
> (352) 493-6072

The Eastern Lake Trail at Point Washington State Forest offers old logging roads for hiking. These double-track roads provide very sandy riding on the 9-mile loop. Point Washington State Forest is between Destin and Panama City. The trail starts on CR 395, about a mile south of SR 98.

> Contact:
> Florida Division of Forestry
> Point Washington State Forest
> 5865 Highway 98 East
>
> Santa Rosa Beach, FL 32459
> (850) 231-5800

The Fern Trail is a 3.3-mile single-track connecting central Tallahassee with Tom Brown Park. The trail begins at the corner of

Magnolia Dr. and Park Ave. Tom Brown Park has 6 miles of single-track and is located off of Capital Circle East.

Contact:
Tom Brown Park
(850) 891-3965

St. Marks National Wildlife Refuge is a 65,000-acre refuge that has impoundment dikes cyclists can ride on. Located south of Newport on SR 50, this area allows seasonal hunting.
Contact:
U.S. Fish and Wildlife Service
P.O. Box 68
St. Marks, FL 32355
(850) 925-6121

Hickory Mound Impoundment in the Big Bend Wildlife Management Area offers hiking on the 6.5-mile dike surrounding the impoundment. It is located 18 miles west of Perry on US 98.
Contact:
Florida Fish and Wildlife Conservation Commission
Big Bend WMA Field Office
663 Plantation Road
Perry, FL 32347
(850) 838-9016

Andrews Wildlife Management Area, an 800-acre hardwood hammock, has several narrow, unmaintained roads that are suitable for hiking. Maps can be found at the kiosk near the entrance, which is located on CR 211, 5 miles north of Chiefland. Hunting is allowed in season.
Contact:
Florida Fish and Wildlife Conservation Commission
Andrews WMA Field Office
Route 1, Box 741
Trenton, FL 32693
(352) 493-6020

Tyndall Air Force Base is 10 miles southeast of Panama City on US 98. Biking is allowed on several miles of sandy dirt roads.
Contact:
Natural Resources Office
Tyndall Air Force Base, FL 32403
(850) 283-2641

Lines Tract Trail is an off-road bike trail located in Lake Talquin State Forest west of Tallahassee. The forest also contains additional forest roads through varying terrain.
Contact:
Lake Talquin State Forest
(850) 488-1871

SOME ALABAMA OFF-ROAD TRAILS

Chickasabogue Park offers 10 miles of single-track loops that fall into the moderate to difficult category. This county park charges an entry fee and is located off I-65 approximately 12 miles north of Mobile, Alabama.
Contact:
Chickasabogue Park
760 Aldock Road
Mobile, AL 36613
(251)574-2267

Conecuh Trail in the Conecuh National Forest has a 10-mile loop of easy, wide single-track. The forest is approximately 90 miles northeast of Pensacola, off FL 189, which becomes AL 137 at the border. Hunting is allowed in season, and maps can be purchased from the ranger's office in Andalusia, Alabama.
Contact:
National Forest District Ranger Office
Route 5, Box 157
Andalusia, AL 36420
(334) 222-2555

Chattahoochee State Park is a small park that offers 6 miles of looping jeep roads and 4 miles of fire roads. The park is located north of Marianna, Florida, on AL 95.

Contact:
Chattahoochee State Park
Star Route, Box 108
Cordon, AL 36343
(334) 522-3607

BICYCLE CLUBS OF NORTHWEST FLORIDA

Capital City Cyclists
P.O. Box 4222
Tallahassee, FL 32315-4222
Hotline: (850) 847-8433
Website: www.cccyclists.org

Emerald Coast Cyclists
P.O. Box 592
Niceville, FL 32588
Hotline: (850) 864-7166
Contact: John Stamp
(850) 897-6862
Website: www.eccyclists.com
Interests: road, off-road, racing, safety/education
Annual events: late September/early October road race

Panama City Flyers
P.O. Box 15966
Panama City, FL 32406-5966
Contact: Henry Lawrence
(850) 258-1276
Annual events: Tour de Ranch (25, 62.5, and 100 miles), held in March; Fall Classic Omnium time-trial, road race, and criterium, held in the fall

Pensacola Freewheelers Bicycle Club
Contact: Larry Brown, President
(850) 944-4163
Interests: weekly road rides

Northeast

Website: www.pensacolafreewheelers.com

Mention northeast Florida and most people will immediately think of the metropolis of Jacksonville. But while Jacksonville has much to offer and has given us such musical talent as Pat Boone, Slim Whitman (the term talent is used loosely here), Lynyrd Skynyrd, and Marcus Roberts, it is certainly not all that northeast Florida has to offer. There is also Gainesville, widely recognized as the state's most bike-friendly city, and its little neighbor, Micanopy, which has proclaimed itself Florida's oldest inland town. And don't forget historic and picturesque St. Augustine, the oldest continuous European settlement in the United States.

The terrain in the Northeast consists mainly of gently rolling hills inland and flat, sandy lowlands at the coast. While the hills here can be significant, they are generally not as eminent (some flatlanders might say "ominous") as those in either northwest or central Florida. Off-roaders will be happy to hear that although the soil can be somewhat sandy in this part of the state, all of the rides listed in this chapter should be manageable for riders of nearly all abilities. Roadies will enjoy the variety provided by the proximity of the rolling hills to the long stretches of flat coastal highway.

In winter, the climate of the Northeast is, of course, a bit cooler than balmy south Florida. The lows usually bottom out in the low 40s, with infrequent dips down below freezing. The average winter highs are in the low to mid 60s. The summer temperatures are very similar to those in the rest of the state, with average lows in the low 70s and highs in the low 90s. Spring and autumn offer the best opportunities for riding, with their combination of mild temperatures and relatively little precipitation. The average yearly rainfall of 51 inches is also about average for the rest of the state. The majority of this comes from the regular summer deluges, which actually can be quite welcome and refreshing on a sweltering afternoon. Just pack a rain jacket and watch out for the lightning.

Most of the cycling activity here centers around Gainesville and Jacksonville. There is plenty of recreational riding and racing to keep people fit, fast, and on their bikes year-round. As far as organized cycling goes, one of the most notable features of the Northeast region is that group of hard-working, trail-blazing fun hogs known as the Suwannee Bicycle Association. This gang is responsible for the creation of more official off-road bike trails than any other organization in the state. They also organize some top-notch annual events, including the Suwannee Bicycle Festival, a springtime road ride extravaganza, and their fall Florida Fat-Tire Festival, the largest off-road event in the Sunshine State. If you are looking for places to ride in northeast Florida, first try some of the rides in this chapter. If you get done with all of them and are still hungry for more, call the Suwannee Bicycle Association (their number is listed at the end of this section). They can load you down with enough information to fill another book.

ROAD RIDES

DOWLING PARK LOOP

Location: Suwannee River State Park, Ellaville
Distance: 33 miles
Terrain: mostly flat with a few small hills
Description: This road loop leaves from Suwannee River State Park and visits the small community of Dowling Park. Along the way, it travels mostly quiet roads with a few very mild grades. There is some—but not a lot—of shade along the route. However, the return trip does offer an opportunity for a refreshing dip in Falmouth Spring—a wonderful way to cool off on a hot day In addition to being just plain fun to swim in, the spring is also interesting because it flows only about 400 feet as a river, then disappears underground and is never seen again.

Fees: $4 entry fee for Suwannee River State Park

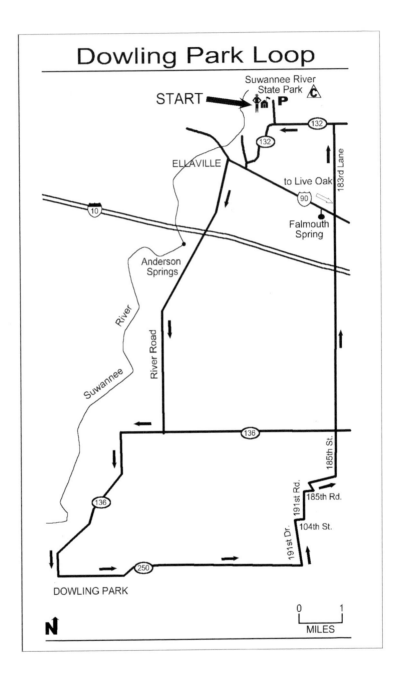

Dowling Park Loop

Facilities: There are rest rooms, water, picnic tables, camping, and hiking trails at Suwannee River State Park. There is also a toilet at Falmouth Spring.

Finding the ride: From I-10's exit 275, head west on US 90 for 5 miles and turn right at the entrance to Suwannee River State Park in Ellaville. Follow the park drive for 0.5 mile and park in the lot near the office.

Mileage log

0.0	Exit the park on the road you came in on.
0.1	Turn right onto US 90 at the stop sign.
1.0	Turn left onto River Road.
2.8	Cross the I-10 overpass.
7.6	Turn right onto CR 136 at the stop sign.
8.6	Follow the ninety-degree left curve in the road.
12.0	Go right into Dowling Park.
12.4	Turn left onto CR 250 at the red flashing light.
18.1	Turn left onto 191st Dr., just after passing Clayland Church on your right.
19.2	Turn right onto 104th St.
19.3	Turn left onto 191st Rd.
20.0	Turn right onto 185th Rd.
20.1	Follow the ninety-degree left curve.
21.9	Go straight across CR 136 at the stop sign.
23.4	Go straight across 76th St. at the stop sign.
25.5	Cross the I-10 overpass.
26.8	Turn left onto US 90 at the stop sign.
27.0	Turn left at the entrance to Falmouth Spring. There is swimming, picnic tables, and a toilet here. Head back out to US 90 when you are done.
27.4	Those who have worn themselves out frolicking in the spring can turn left onto US 90 and find their way back to the park in about 2 miles. Those who want to get in a few more pleasant, shady miles should turn right onto US 90 and follow the remaining instructions.
27.6	Turn left onto 183rd Ln.
29.7	Turn left onto CR 132 at the stop sign.
32.4	At this stop sign, turn right into the park entrance.
32.9	You are back in the parking lot, near the office.

For more information, contact:
Suwannee River State Park
20185 CR 132
Live Oak, FL 32060
(386) 362-2746

SUWANNEE SPRINGS LOOP

Location: White Springs
Distance: 31 miles
Terrain: mildly hilly
Description: This ride starts in charming White Springs, home
of the prolific Suwannee Bicycle Association, and visits the legendary
healing powers of Suwannee Springs. The route parallels the Suwannee
River, heading out along its southern banks and returning along the
northern side. It travels mainly quiet farm roads with miles and miles
of cotton fields punctuated by the occasional grazing cow. The spring
and the ruins of the old springhouse that once surrounded it are a
lovely spot for a rest stop. The water is always cool and inviting for a
swim. Some find its sulfurous smell off-putting, but if the weather is
hot enough, most people are willing to plug their noses and hop in

The old spring house at Suwannee Springs

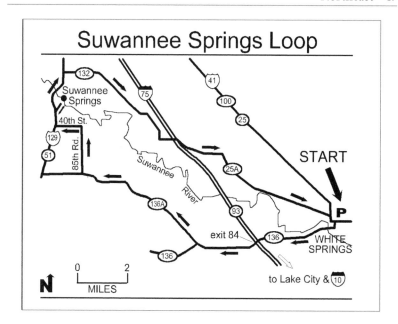

Suwannee Springs Loop

for a refreshing dip.

Fees: none

Facilities: There are a couple of convenience stores in White Springs and one near Suwannee Springs.

Finding the ride: From I-75's exit 439, take CR 136 3.2 miles east into White Springs. Go straight across US 41 at the red flashing light. The Suwannee Bicycle Association office is a half block down Bridge St., on the right. You can park on the street there. Be sure to stop at the bike association office and say hey if anyone is around. They are a bunch of nice people and have all kinds of information on other places to ride—both on and off-road—in this area.

Mileage log

0.0	Starting from the S.B.A. headquarters, cross US 41 and head west on CR 136.
0.1	Cross the Suwannee River.
3.2	Cross the I-75 overpass.
5.6	Cross the bridge over Rocky Creek.
5.7	Turn right onto CR 136A.
11.4	Turn right onto 85th Rd.
13.2	Turn left onto 40th St.
14.3	At the stop sign, turn right onto US 129.

14.9	After the convenience store and before the agricultural inspection station, turn right onto 93rd Dr.
15.2	Turn right onto the dirt 32nd St. at the brown sign for Suwannee Springs.
15.5	You are at the spring parking lot. There is a toilet and some picnic tables here. To get down to the spring, follow the cement walk off to your left. Mmm! Can you smell that healing power? Head back out the way you came when you are done here.
15.9	Turn left onto 93rd Dr. at the stop sign.
16.2	At the stop sign, turn right onto US 129.
17.3	Cross the bridge over the Suwannee River.
17.9	Turn right onto CR 132.
18.3	You are now going up the toughest climb of the ride.
19.5	Turn right onto CR 25A.
22.3	The highway at your right is I-75.
23.7	Cross the I-75 overpass.
27.1	Cross the bridge over Swift Creek.
29.0	Cross the bridge over Sal Marie Branch.
30.3	Go straight at the stop sign.
30.6	Turn right at the stop sign.
30.7	Follow the ninety-degree left turn in the road.
31.0	At the stop sign, turn right onto US 41.
31.3	Turn left onto Bridge St. at the yellow flashing light, and you are done.

For more information, contact:
Suwannee Bicycle Association
P.O. Box 247
White Springs, FL 32096-0247
(386) 397-2347
Website: http://www.suwanneebike.org
Contact: Kim Frawley, President
woodbike@bellsouth.net

PENNEY FARMS

Location: Jacksonville

Distance: 51 miles

Terrain: mildly hilly

Description: This ride allows you to pedal away from the urban sprawl and out into the rolling countryside southwest of Jacksonville. It departs from Grove Park, located in Orange Park, on the south side of the city. The first and last 5 miles ply mostly quiet neighborhood streets. The next few miles may be busy with traffic, especially during the work week, but the roads are generally safe for cycling. Once away from the city, the riding becomes much more peaceful. The section of SR 16 that travels through Penney Farms is so gorgeous that it will leave you wondering why all roads aren't made that way. This route also serves up a slice of north Florida culture, with a pass by Ronnie Van Zant Memoria Park, named in honor of one of the founding members of the southern rock group Lynyrd Skynyrd. Van Zant died along with two other members of the band in a tragic plane crash in 1977.

Fees: none

Facilities: There are rest rooms and water at Grove Park. There are plenty of places to stop for other essentials along the route.

Finding the ride: From the I-295/US 17 interchange at exit 10, take US 17 south for 1.7 miles and turn right onto Kingsley Ave. for 1

Peaceful pedaling (Penney Farms)

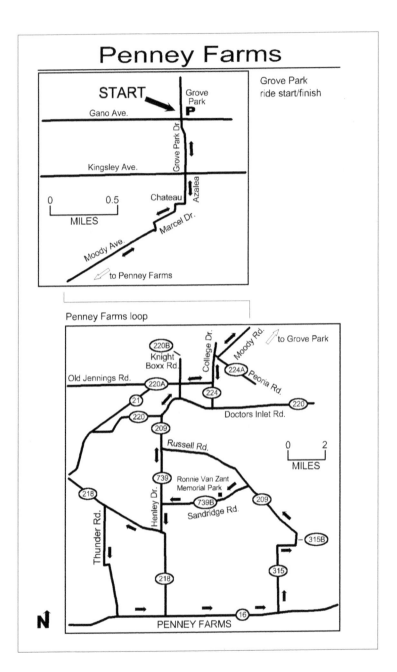

Penney Farms

START ← Grove Park

Gano Ave.

Grove Park Dr.

Kingsley Ave.

Chateau

Azalea

Marcel Dr.

Moody Ave.

0   0.5

MILES

to Penney Farms

Grove Park
ride start/finish

P

Penney Farms loop

220B Knight Boxx Rd.

College Dr.

Moody Rd.

to Grove Park

Old Jennings Rd.

220A

224A Peoria Rd.

21

224

220

220

Doctors Inlet Rd.

209

Russell Rd.

0   2

MILES

739

Ronnie Van Zant
Memorial Park

218

Henley Dr.

739B

Sandridge Rd.

209

Thunder Rd.

315B

218

315

N

16

PENNEY FARMS

mile. Turn right onto Grove Park Dr. for 0.4 mile. Turn right onto Grove Ave. then left into the parking lot at Grove Park.

Mileage log

0.0	From the parking lot near the tennis courts at Grove Park, turn right onto Gano Ave.
0.1	Turn left onto Grove Park Dr.
0.5	Cross Kingsley Ave. (use caution). You are now on Azalea Ln.
0.7	Turn right onto Chateau, then immediately left onto Marcel Dr.
1.0	Turn left onto Moody Ave. There is a separate bike path along much of this road.
4.9	Turn right at the stop sign onto Peoria Rd. (CR 224A).
5.2	Turn left at the traffic light onto College Dr. (CR 224). There is a bike lane along here that you can use.
6.3	Turn right at the traffic light onto Old Jennings Rd. (CR 220A).
7.6	Turn left at the traffic light onto Knight Boxx Rd. (CR 220B).
8.2	Turn right at the traffic light onto Doctors Inlet Rd. (CR 220).
9.3	Turn left at the traffic light onto Russell Rd. (CR 209).
10.3	Cross the bridge over Block Creek.
10.7	Turn right onto Henley Dr. (CR 739).
14.1	Turn right at the stop sign onto CR 218.
16.6	Turn left onto Thunder Rd.
19.0	Turn left at the stop sign (still on Thunder Rd.).
19.1	Follow the ninety-degree right turn (still on Thunder Rd.).
21.2	Turn left at the stop sign onto SR 16.
21.6	Enter Penney Farms. Is this not a beautiful section of road?
27.9	Turn left onto CR 315.
30.6	Turn right (still on CR 315).
31.3	Turn left onto CR 31 SB.
31.9	Just before crossing the railroad tracks, turn left onto Russell Rd. (CR 209).
34.6	Turn left onto Sandridge Rd. (CR 739B).
37.5	On your left is Ronnie Van Zant Memorial Park, a good place for a rest if you need one. Do not be surprised if you find yourself humming "Sweet Home Alabama" the rest of the way back.
38.4	Turn right at the stop sign onto Henley Dr. (CR 739).

40.7	Turn left at the stop sign onto Russell Rd. (CR 209).
42.1	Turn right at the traffic light onto Doctors Inlet Rd.(CR 220).
43.2	Turn left at the traffic light onto Knight Boxx Rd.
43.8	Turn right at the traffic light onto Old Jennings Rd.
45.1	Turn left at the traffic light onto College Dr. (CR 224).
46.2	Turn right at the traffic light onto Peoria Rd.
46.5	Turn left onto Moody Ave.
50.4	Turn right onto Marcel Dr.
50.7	Turn right onto Chateau, then immediately left onto Azalea Ln.
50.9	Use caution crossing Kingsley Ave.
51.3	Turn right at the stop sign onto Gano Ave.
51.4	Turn left into Grove Park, and you are done.

For more information, contact:
North Florida Bicycle Club
P.O. Box 380082
Jacksonville, FL 32205
Hotline: (904) 721-5870
Website: www.nfbc.us

MANDARIN LOLLIPOP

Location: Jacksonville
Distance: 27 miles
Terrain: mostly flat
Description: This popular route consists of a 13-mile loop on the end of a 7-mile stretch that is ridden out and back. The loop travels mostly quiet, shady neighborhood streets. The first and last few miles, along San Jose Blvd., can have quite a bit of traffic, but cyclists can take advantage of the wide parking lane that rarely has many cars in it. The ride starts and ends in the parking lot at Open Road Bicycles.
Fees: none
Facilities: There are no public rest rooms along the route, but there are several places to stop for food and drink.
Finding the ride: From I-95's exit 106, take Atlantic Blvd. west

Mandarin Lollipop

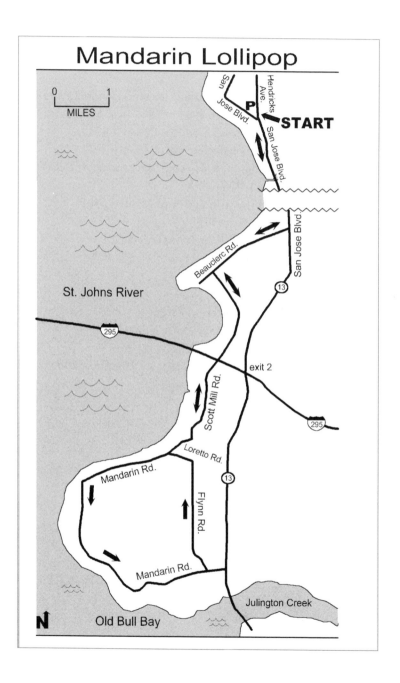

for 0.5 mile. Turn left at the traffic light onto Hendricks Ave. for 2.2 miles. The parking lot for Open Road Bicycles is on your right, next to Blockbuster Video.

Mileage log

0.0	Turn right out of the parking lot onto Hendricks Ave. Its name changes to San Jose Blvd. in about a block
5.0	Cross the bridge over Goodbys Creek
5.3	Turn right onto Beauclerc Rd.
6.7	Turn left at the three-way stop sign onto Scott Mill Rd
8.2	Cross under 1-295.
9.5	Turn right at the stop sign onto Mandarin Rd
14.6	Turn left onto Flynn Rd.
16.3	Turn left at the stop sign onto Loretto Rd
16.7	Turn right at the stop sign onto Mandarin Rd
17.2	Turn left onto Scott Mill Rd.
18.5	Pass under I-295 again.
20.0	Turn right at the three-way stop sign onto Beauclerc Rd
21.4	Turn left at the stop sign onto San Jose Blvd
21.7	Cross Goodbye Creek again.
26.7	Turn left into the parking lot at the bike shop, and you are done.

For more information, contact:
North Florida Bicycle Club
P.O. Box 380082
Jacksonville, FL 32205
Hotline: (904) 721-5870
Website: www.nfbc.com

JACKSONVILLE BEACH TO PONTE VEDRA BEACH

Location: Jacksonville
Distance: 19 miles
Terrain: flat
Description: This pleasant out-and-back beach ride departs from Jacksonville Beach and heads south along the coast to Ponte Vedra Beach. The Jacksonville area is loaded with interesting shops, cafés

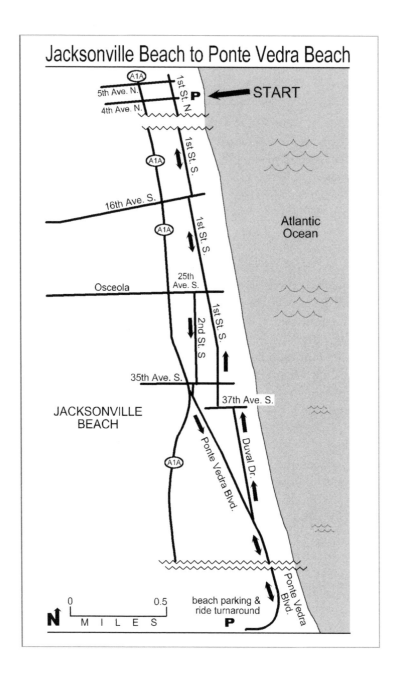

Jacksonville Beach to Ponte Vedra Beach

A1A
5th Ave. N.
1st St. N
P ← START
4th Ave. N.

1st St. S.
A1A
16th Ave. S.

Atlantic
Ocean

A1A
1st St. S.

25th
Ave. S.
Osceola
1st St. S.

2nd St. S
35th Ave. S.
37th Ave. S.

JACKSONVILLE
BEACH
A1A
Ponte Vedra Blvd.
Duval Dr.

beach parking &
ride turnaround
P
Ponte Vedra Blvd.

0   0.5
N   M I L E S

and eateries, and the area can be quite busy with both pedestrian and automobile traffic. There are stop signs every few blocks for the first few miles of the route, which not only facilitate the flow of traffic, but also serve to moderate your pace so you can look around and pick out the places you want to patronize when you return.

Ponte Vedra Beach is an upper-crust area full of fancy homes and private country clubs. There will not be many rednecks hurling empty cans of cheap beer out their car windows in this neighborhood. Ponte Vedra Blvd. is flat and straight. With a posted speed limit of 25 to 35 miles per hour, it is a good place to work on your time trialing, do intervals, or just get lost in your own thoughts and enjoy the scenery. In between the houses you can even catch glimpses of the deep blue Atlantic on one side of the road and the rapidly disappearing marshy wetlands on the other.

Fees: You may need to feed a parking meter, depending on where you park.

Facilities: There are rest rooms, water, and showers available at the beach parking area, where the ride starts. There are also plenty of restaurants and shops in the vicinity.

Finding the ride: From I-95's exit 106, take Atlantic Blvd. east for 15.6 miles. Turn right onto 3rd St. N. (SR A1A) for 2.3 miles. Turn left onto 5th Ave. N. and go 2 blocks to the beach parking lot on 1st St. N., between 4th and 5th Ave. N.

Mileage log

0.0	Turn left out of the beach parking lot onto 1st St. N.
0.4	Cross Beach Blvd. You are now on 1st St. S.
1.4	Turn right at the stop sign onto 16th Ave. S., then immediately turn left onto 1st St. S.
1.8	Turn right onto 25th Ave. S. at the stop sign.
1.9	Turn left onto 2nd St. S.
2.3	At the stop sign, make a right turn onto 35th Ave. S., then immediately turn left (before you get to the traffic light) onto the small, unmarked street.
2.4	Turn left onto Ponte Vedra Blvd. at the stop sign.
3.0	Enter Ponte Vedra Beach.
9.4	Ponte Vedra Blvd. makes a sweeping right curve here. Turn left into the parking lot, which is the turnaround point and also a nice place to stop and visit the beach. When you are done, turn right onto Ponte Vedra Blvd.

15.8	Turn right onto Duval Dr.
16.3	At the stop sign, turn left onto 37th Ave. S.
16.4	Turn right onto 1st St. S. at the stop sign.
17.3	Make a right turn onto 16th Ave. S. at the stop sign, then immediately turn left onto 1st St. S.
18.3	Cross Beach Blvd. You are now on 1st St. N.
18.7	Turn right into the beach parking lot, and you are done.

For more information, contact:
North Florida Bicycle Club
P.O. Box 380082
Jacksonville, FL 32205
Hotline: (904) 721-5870
Website: www.nfbc.com

ANASTASIA A1A

Location: St. Augustine Beach
Distance: 24 miles
Terrain: flat
Description: This is a nice out-and-back ride for hammer-heads that just want to haul booty along the flat coastal highway. But it is an even better ride for those who like to stop and smell the roses along the way. It departs from Frank Butler Park, just south of St. Augustine. The route offers riders a chance to take a free boat ride over to Rattlesnake Island for a visit to Fort Matanzas National Monument. This is the small outpost that guarded the "backdoor" entry to St. Augustine's famous Castillo de San Marcos. It is also the site of the 1565 massacre of nearly three hundred French Huguenots by the Spaniards. Hence the name matanzas, which is Spanish for "slaughters." The turnaround point for the ride is at Washington Oaks Gardens State Park, a lovely place for a rest, perhaps a picnic, and a stroll through the lush gardens. As with most of the rest of A1A, this section can be subject to strong crosswinds ripping in off the Atlantic, so leave your disc wheels at home.

Fees: There is a small entry fee (<$5) if you choose to visit Washington Oaks Gardens State Park.

Facilities: There are rest rooms, water, showers, beach access, and

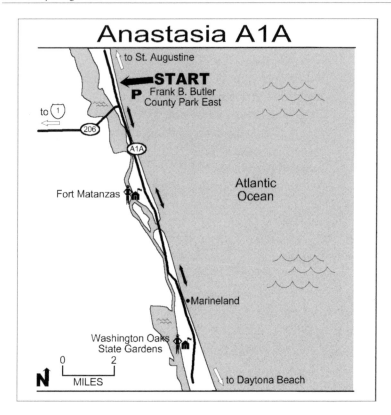

picnic areas at the starting/ending point There are also facilities at Washington Oaks Gardens State Park (fee) and Fort Matanzas National Monument (free).

Finding the ride: From St. Augustine, take SR A1A (Anastasia Blvd) south. About 2.5 miles south of the point where A1A and CR 3 merge, turn left into Frank Butler Park. The ride starts from there.

Mileage log

0.0	Turn left onto SR A1A from the parking lot at Frank Butler Park East.
1.2	Pass SR 206, which is on your right.
5.2	On your right is the entrance to Fort Matanzas National Monument. There are facilities there if you need them.
6.0	You are crossing over the Matanzas Inlet.
8.6	Marineland is on your left.
11.4	Turn right at the entrance to Washington Oaks Gardens State Park.

11.6	Pay a small fee at the entry station.
11.7	Turn left at the stop sign.
11.9	The gardens are off to your right, and there is a place to park and lock your bike on the left. A picnic area is 0.3 mile further down the road. When you are ready, head back the way you came.
12.2	Turn right, back toward the entry station.
12.5	Turn left onto SR A1A.
15.3	There is Marineland again, on your right.
17.9	Cross back over Matanzas Inlet.
18.7	Your last chance for that boat ride over to Fort Matanzas is on your left.
22.7	Pass SR 206, which is on your left.
23.9	Turn right into the parking lot at Frank Butler Park East, and you are done.

For more information contact:
Washington Oaks Gardens State Park
6400 N. Oceanshore Blvd.
Palm Coast, FL 32137
(386) 446-6780
or
Fort Matanzas National Monument
(904) 471-0116

GAINESVILLE-HAWTHORNE STATE TRAIL TO MICANOPY

Location: Gainesville
Distance: 30 miles
Terrain: mildly rolling
Description: The 17-mile Gainesville-Hawthorne State Trail is just one of the many reasons that Gainesville is often considered to be Florida's most bike-friendly city. Its many miles of roads with paved shoulders and bike lanes make getting around the city on two wheels a breeze. The state trail is used mostly for recreation and not

On the road to Micanopy

transportation, since its current trailhead is located on the southeast side of town, several miles from the hustle and bustle of the University of Florida campus and the business district. One day the trail may be tied in with Gainesville's extensive bike path network, but for now it is still relatively easy to reach either by car or bicycle. The trail travels the path of an old railroad bed, skirting along the northern edge of Payne's Prairie, through the small communities of Rochelle and Grove Park, and terminating in Hawthorne. The trail itself is easy to follow, and you really do not need any specific directions. This ride, however, offers an interesting side trip off the trail to the charming, historic town of Micanopy, which offers distinctive, and increasingly rare, Florida ambiance. Now renowned for its art galleries and antiques shops, Micanopy is said to be Florida's oldest inland settlement.

Fees: none

Facilities: There are rest rooms and water at the trailhead. Micanopy has a couple places to make a pit stop and get a cold drink.

Finding the ride: From the intersection of 13th St. (US 441) and University Ave. (SR 26) in Gainesville, head east on University Ave. for 1.8 miles and turn right onto SE 15th St. for 2 miles. Turn right into the second driveway at Boulware Springs Park, then make an immediate right to park in the grassy parking area that is specifically designated as trailhead parking.

Mileage Log

0.0	Turn right out of the grassy trailhead parking area onto the paved park road and go down the hill. Follow the signs for the trail.
0.2	Turn left onto the paved road.
0.3	Turn right and you are on the trail.
1.0	Sweetwater Branch Overlook offers a view of Paynes Prairie.
1.2	There is a restroom just off the trail on your right.
1.6	The La Chua Trail, on your right, is an unpaved trail into Paynes Prairie.

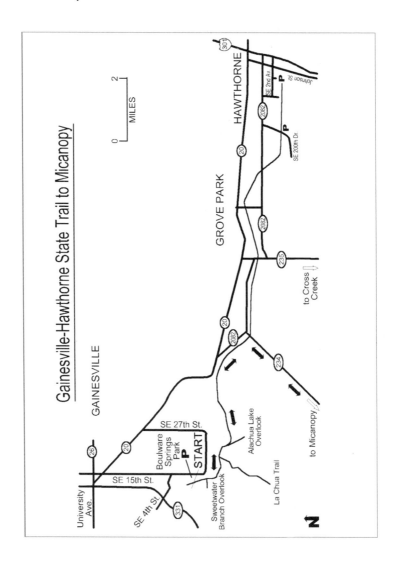

2.1	Take the left branch at this fork. The right-hand path leads to an overlook of Alachua Lake.
6.7	This is where you will leave the trail and head to Micanopy. Turn right onto CR 234 at the stop sign.
8.6	Cross a small bridge.
13.6	Cross US 441 at the yellow flashing light. There are a couple of convenience stores at this intersection.
14.1	Here is downtown Micanopy. Take your time to explore and enjoy. There are some interesting homes with pretty yards in the neighborhood off of this main street. When you are done here, head back out of town the way you came.
14.6	Cross back over US 441 at the yellow flashing light.
21.5	Turn left back onto the trail just before CR 2082.
27.9	You are back at the trailhead. Turn left.
30.0	Turn right onto the paved path.
30.1	If you have not yet had a look at Boulware Spring, pull off to the right and check it out.
30.2	Turn left into the parking area, and you are done.

For more information contact:
Gainesville Bicycle/Pedestrian Program
P.O. Box 490, MS 28
Gainesville, FL 32602-0490
(352) 334-5074

OFF-ROAD RIDES

ANDERSON SPRINGS

Location: Twin Rivers State Forest, Ellaville (halfway between Tallahassee and Jacksonville)
Distance: 7 miles
Terrain: moderate to difficult single-track
Description: This is a tight, 4.3-mile single-track that undulates along the bank of the Suwannee River. There are no real hills to speak of, but there are enough short rises and drops to keep things interesting.

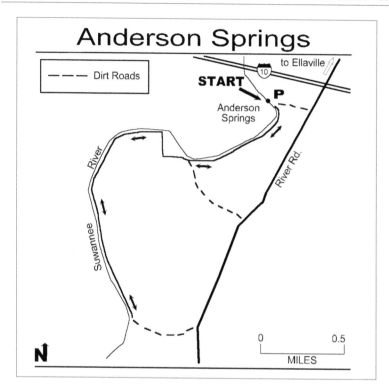

You will find yourself pedaling among stands of saw palmettos and various oaks covered with lichen and strewn with vines and Spanish moss. Wild turkeys are not uncommon here, and large spiders and their icky-sticky webs are downright abundant. Caution: There is seasonal hunting in the Twin Rivers State Forest.

Fees: none

Facilities: There are no facilities at the trailhead. Ellaville, 2 miles north, should be able to supply the basics.

Finding the ride: From US 90 in Ellaville, head south on River Rd. You will cross I-10 after 2 miles. Continue 0.3 mile farther south, turn right onto the dirt road, follow it 0.3 mile to the river, and park there. Anderson Springs will be almost right in front of you. You should be able to see it bubbling up if the river is not too high.

Mileage log

0.0   From Anderson Springs, head south on the double-track along the river.

0.2   The double-track turns into single-track.

0.8	The trail turns right and widens a bit.
0.9	Cross a double-track. There is a closed gate off to your right.
2.1	There is a small clearing here. Follow the single-track that continues off to the right.
3.3	This clearing marks the turnaround point. The double-track on your left goes out to River Rd. There is a picnic table by the river on your right. Head back the way you came when you are ready.
4.1	Cross the clearing again.
5.7	Cross the double-track with the closed gate off to your left.
5.8	Turn left off of the wide track onto the narrow single-track.
6.5	The single-track widens to double-track.
6.6	You are back at Anderson Springs.

For more information, contact:
Suwannee Bicycle Association
P.O. Box 247
White Springs, FL 32096-0247
(386) 397-2347
Website: http://www.suwanneebike.org
Contact: Kim Frawley, President
woodbike@bellsouth.net
or
Twin Rivers State Forest
7620 133rd Rd.
Live Oak, FL 32060
(386) 208-1460

HOLTON CREEK

Location: Live Oak
Distance: 16 miles
Terrain: mostly flat double-track
Description: The Holton Creek Tract is public land managed by the Suwannee River Water Management District. The first 2 miles of this ride are quite sandy, but do not let that discourage you. The best is yet to come. The rest of the ride is on a jungly woodland road

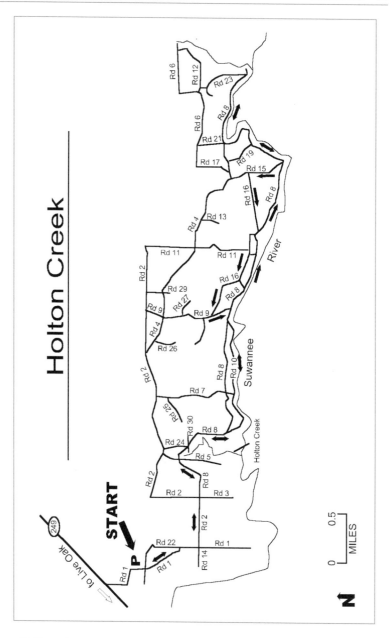

paralleling the Suwannee River, traveling past numerous sinkholes along the way. Wildlife abounds here, especially in the form of the charming, if not too astute, *Dasypus novemcinctus*. At some point in this area's history, someone decided to call it the "land of a thousand sinks," a fitting name. Based on my experience here, I've decided to dub it the "land of a thousand nine-banded armadillos." Caution: This is a wildlife management area, and hunting is allowed in season.

Fees: none

Facilities: There is a toilet, but no drinking water at the trailhead. Live Oak is your best bet for all other services, except for bike repairs, which may require a trip to Jacksonville or Tallahassee.

Finding the ride: From US 90 in Live Oak, take CR 249 north for about 12 miles. Take the second dirt road on the right, 0.2 mile after crossing the Suwannee River, at the HOLTON CREEK WMA sign. Continue for 1.1 miles. Turn right at the second HOLTON CREEK WMA sign for 0.3 mile. Take the left fork at the large brown sign, go another 0.4 mile, and park near the big map/information board.

Mileage log

0.0	From the trailhead at the map/information board, head south on Rd. 1.
0.4	Rd. 22 comes in from the left. Stay to the right, on Rd.
0.6	Turn left onto Rd. 2.
1.1	Go straight at this intersection. You are now on Rd. 8.
1.6	Go straight across Rd. 5.
2.3	Turn right onto Rd. 10 and say goodbye to the sand for a while.
3.1	Pass Rd. 7, which is on your left.
3.7	Go left at the fork. The right branch goes a short way to a river overlook.
3.8	Go straight here, where Rd. 8 merges in from the left and Rd. 10 ends. You are now on Rd. 8 again.
4.0	Pass Rd. 9, which is on your left.
4.8	Stay to the right here, where Rd. 16 comes in on your left.
5.8	Pass Rd. 15, which is on your left.
6.7	Stay to the right here, where Rd. 4 and 21 meet Rd. 8.
7.6	The going gets really sandy if you turn left here onto Rd. 23, so this is your turnaround point. There is a nice place for a rest stop if you turn right and follow it a short way to where Mitchell Creek empties into the Suwannee. When you are ready, head back the way you came on Rd. 8.
8.5	Stay to the left here, where Rd. 4 and 21 meet Rd. 8.
10.4	Turn right onto Rd. 16.
10.6	Stay to the left at the first fork.
10.8	Stay to the right at the second fork.

11.4	Turn left onto Rd. 9.
11.6	Make a right turn onto Rd. 8.
11.8	Turn left onto Rd. 10.
11.9	Stay to the right at the fork.
13.2	Turn left onto Rd. 8.
14.4	Go straight at this intersection. You are now on Rd. 2.
14.9	Turn right onto Rd. 1.
15.1	Take the left fork, staying on Rd. 1.
15.5	You are back at the trailhead.

For more information, contact:
Suwannee River Water Management District
9225 CR 49
Live Oak, FL 32060
(386) 362-1001 or (800) 226-1066

BRIDGE-TO-BRIDGE TRAIL

Location: White Springs, 50 miles west of Jacksonville
Distance: 4 to 7 miles
Terrain: moderate single-track

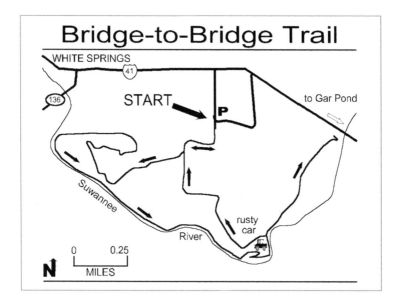

Description: This fine trail, built on public land managed by the Suwannee River Water Management District, is the handiwork of the Suwannee Bicycle Association. Its twisty-turny single-track winds through palmetto thickets along the northern bank of the Suwannee River. Other than a few short rolls, the terrain is mostly flat. However, there are plenty of gatorbacks and other roots to keep you on your toes. The trail is sparsely marked with light-blue blazes, but it is so well bedded in that you do not really need them to find your way.

Fees: none

Facilities: White Springs has all the basics: food, cold drinks, and rest rooms. There is also a small motel and camping is available at Stephen Foster State Folk Culture Center.

Finding the ride: From I-75's exit 439, take CR 136 east for 3.2 miles into White Springs. Just after crossing the Suwannee River, turn right at the red flashing light onto US 41 for 0 7 mile. Turn right onto Adams Memorial Dr. and park in the lot near the ballfields. Ride your bike down Adams Memorial Dr, past the cemetery on your left. You will see the trailhead kiosk straight ahead, where the road makes a ninety-degree left turn.

Mileage Log

0.0	From the kiosk at the trailhead, go south on the double-track.
0.3	Turn right at the BRIDGE-TO-BRIDGE TRAIL sign.
0.6	The double-track ends and the single-track begins. Follow the light-blue blazes.
1.9	Off to the right there is a trail spur that leads to a river over-look.
2.1	Walk your bike through this short section of trail (in order to control erosion).
3.2	The single-track turns into a double-track here. Keep going straight.
3.4	When you get to the intersection at the rusty car you have three choices: 1) Turn around and go back the way you came on the single-track (3.4 miles). 2) Turn left and go back to the trailhead on the double-track (1 mile). 3) Turn right and ride the double-track over to the boat ramp. From here you can ride a short stretch of pavement over to the Gar Pond single-track.

Directions to Gar Pond from the rusty car:

3.4	Turn right at the rusty car.
4.0	At this intersection, turn right and you are at the boat ramp and roadside park. There are some picnic tables and plenty of shade here. Turn left onto the pavement and follow it up the hill.
4.1	Turn right onto US 41 at the stop sign.
4.2	Cross the bridge over the Suwannee River.
4.8	Turn right onto the dirt road at the Discount Liquor Store.
4.9	Here is the trailhead kiosk, just off to your left. See the Gar Pond ride for further instructions.

For more information, contact:
Suwannee Bicycle Association
P.O. Box 247
White Springs, FL 32096-0247
(386) 397-2347
Website: http://www.suwanneebike.org
Contact: Kim Frawley, President
woodbike@bellsouth.net

GAR POND

Location: White Springs, 50 miles west of Jacksonville
Distance: 4 miles
Terrain: moderate single-track
Description: Another of the many Suwannee Bicycle Association trails, the Gar Pond trail is a fast, 4-mile single-track that loops through palmettos and piney woods, visiting a few ponds and sinkholes along the way. For a longer adventure, many riders will want to do this trail in conjunction with its neighbor, the Bridge-to-Bridge Trail. For instructions on how to do so, see the Bridge-to-Bridge ride. This trail is a little easier to ride, and a bit faster.
Fees: none
Facilities: There are no amenities, other than discount liquor, at the trailhead. White Springs has all the basics: food, cold drinks, and rest rooms. There is also a small motel and camping is available at Stephen Foster State Folk Cultural Center.

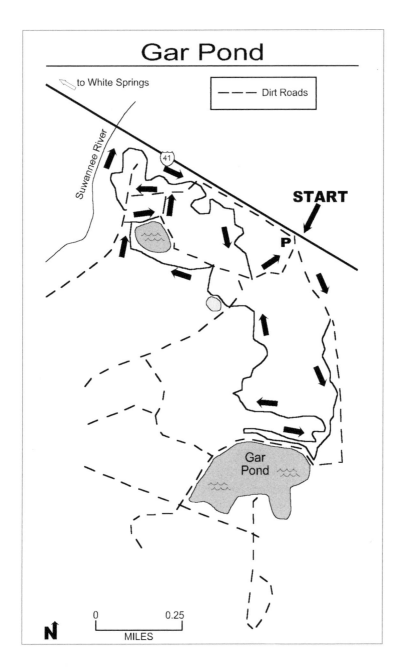

Finding the ride: From I-75's exit 439, take CR 136 east for 3.2 miles
into White Springs. Just after crossing the Suwannee River, turn right

at the flashing red light onto US 41 for 2.0 miles. After crossing the Suwannee again, turn right onto the dirt road at the Discount Liquor Store. You will then see the trailhead kiosk just off to your left. Park near it.

Mileage log

0.0	From the trailhead kiosk, go around the cable blocking the dirt roadway and head south (away from the highway) on the double-track.
0.2	Turn right onto the single-track at the GAR POND TRAIL sign.
0.5	Cross a double-track.
0.7	Gar Pond is off to your left.
1.8	Cross another double-track.
1.9	There is a small pond off to your left.
2.1	There is a larger pond off to your right, which the trail circles around clockwise.
2.4	Now you are heading away from the pond.
2.5	Cross a double-track.
2.8	The trail makes a sharp right-hand turn out near the highway.
2.9	There is a small depression here filled with cypress knees. Be careful. A fall onto one of those babies could really ruin your day.
3.1	Cross a double-track.
3.7	Check out that deep sink off to your right.
3.8	Turn left onto the double-track.
3.9	You are back at the trailhead.

For more information, contact:
Suwannee Bicycle Association
P.O. Box 247
White Springs, FL 32096-0247
(386) 397-2347
Website: http://www.suwanneebike.org
Contact: Kim Frawley, President
woodbike@bellsouth.net

FORT CLINCH STATE PARK

Location: Fernandina Beach
Distance: 6 miles
Terrain: moderate to difficult single-track
Description: The trail at Fort Clinch State Park is a fairly technical single-track that winds through the thick tangled woods on either side of the main park drive. It has a lot of short ups and downs, some of them surprisingly steep, made even more challenging by exposed roots and loose sand. The sand can be bothersome in places, but it is not nearly as bad as one might expect from a trail so close to the beach. There are no blazes marking the trail; you do not need them. The trail is well worn and easy to follow. This is a relatively safe place to ride off-road, because the trail never strays very far from the pavement. Help is nearly always just a shout away. The park also has a 3-mile paved trail for biking.

Fees: <$5 entry fee per vehicle

Facilities: There are rest rooms and water at the park visitors center. The park also offers camping, fishing, and beach access, with showers available at the easternmost beach parking area.

Finding the ride: The entrance to Fort Clinch State Park is on the north side of Atlantic Ave. (SR A1A) in Fernandina Beach, just 1 block

It's not hard to follow the trail. (Ft. Clinch State Park)

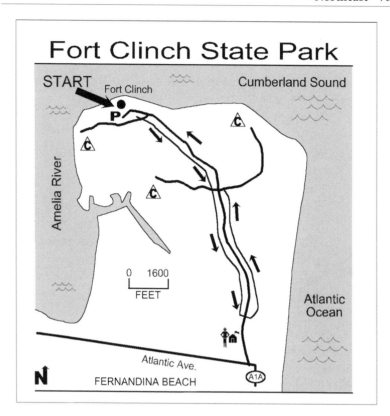

Fort Clinch State Park

START
Fort Clinch
Cumberland Sound
P
Amelia River
0   1600
FEET
Atlantic
Ocean
Atlantic Ave.
N
FERNANDINA BEACH
A1A

inland from the Atlantic Ocean. The trailhead is in the visitors center parking lot, 3 miles north of the entrance station. Turn left immediately upon reaching the parking lot and park near the big gray trail sign. For those who would rather save a couple of bucks by hiking into the park instead of driving, there is a public park where you can leave your car 0.4 mile farther inland from the state park entrance.

Mileage log

0.0	Head into the woods on the single-track next to the big gray bike trail sign.
0.2	Use caution crossing the paved road.
0.3	You have two options here: Go right to go through a steep ditch or go left to avoid the steep ditch. Both trails meet up in a short distance.
0.9	Continue straight across this dirt parking area. The Willow Pond Trail, off to your right, is for hikers only.
1.4	Cross a dirt road.

2.0	Continue straight across this small parking area.
2.4	Cross a small clearing.
2.5	Take the right branch at this fork.
3.0	The trail crosses the main park road here (be careful) and heads back north, toward the visitors center.
3.5	Turn right onto the paved road where the single-track comes out.
3.6	Turn right, back into the woods, where the single-track resumes.
3.7	Turn right onto the paved road again.
3.8	Turn right into the woods, on the single-track again.
4.8	Turn left onto this paved road, then right at the stop sign onto the main park road. Head back up the pavement to the parking lot.
5.8	Stay to the right at the fork.
6.0	You are back at the trailhead.

For more information, contact:
Fort Clinch State Park
2601 Atlantic Ave.
Fernandina Beach, FL 32034
(904) 277-7274

HANNA PARK

Location: Jacksonville
Distance: 9 miles
Terrain: moderate to difficult single-track
Description: The trail network at Kathryn Abbey Hanna Park is a textbook example of how to cram the maximum amount of single-track into a minimal space. These trails zigzag through the woods, switching back upon themselves again and again, so that there is nary a straight line to be seen. There are actually sixteen different sections of trail, with varying degrees of difficulty, sporting colorful names like "Dead Dog," "Misery," and "Devil Stick." These sections may be linked together in various combinations to provide custom-tailored rides of

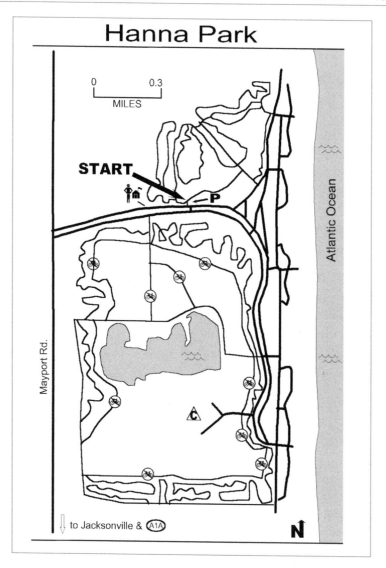

various lengths and difficulty levels. It does get sandy in places, but never for too long a stretch. There are a few small slopes, with plenty of exposed roots and tight turns on the more challenging sections.

Fees: park entry fee <$5

Facilities: Water, rest rooms, camping, and beach access are available at the park.

Finding the ride: From central Jacksonville, take Atlantic Blvd. (SR 10) east for about 13 miles and turn left onto Mayport Rd. (SR A1A). 2.1 miles farther, where A1A turns left, continue straight (north) on

Mayport Rd. Continue 1 mile farther and turn right onto Wonderwood Dr. at the HANNA PARK sign. From the entrance station, drive into the park for 0.1 mile and make a U-turn at the BIKER PARKING sign. Go just a short way and park on the grass on the right-hand side of the road in the biker parking area. The trail begins in the woods near where you just U-turned.

Mileage log: Because of the complexity and flexibility of this trail network, no detailed mileage log has been included here. Riders can get a trail map at the entrance or simply pedal onto the trail and start exploring. The map helps a lot, though, especially in choosing trails that are appropriate for one's skill level. Keep in mind, too, that none of the trails here are really easy, nor are any extremely difficult. It is nearly as impossible to get lost here as it is to not have fun.

For more information, contact:
Hanna Park
500 Wonderwood Dr.
Jacksonville, FL 32233
(904) 249-4700

GUANA TOLOMATO MATANZAS NATIONAL ESTUARINE RESEARCH RESERVE (GTMNERR)

Location: Ponte Vedra Beach, 20 miles south of Jacksonville and 10 miles north of St. Augustine

Distance: 9 miles

Terrain: flat double-track

Description: Some riders might be tempted to put it in the big ring and fly along this wide, hard-packed route at warp speed. To do so might be fun, but not nearly as worthwhile as adopting a more moderate pace and savoring the beauty of this lovely bit of wilderness. With a quiet and cautious approach, sightings of deer, wild pigs, armadillos, raccoons, quail, wild turkeys, and various other woodland animals and waterfowl are quite probable. Pay particularly close attention around the several small ponds and watering holes. These are popular wildlife hangouts.

Fees: $3 entry fee at the self-service pay station.

Facilities: Rest rooms and water are available near the trailhead.

They are on your right as you enter, just after the pay station and before the parking area.

Finding the ride: From Jacksonville, take SR A1A about 20 miles south to South Ponte Vedra Beach. Turn right onto the dirt road at the signs for GTM ENVIRONMENTAL EDUCATION CENTER, GUANA DAM USE AREA, and GUANA RIVER WILDLIFE MGMT. AREA. The parking area is just a short way past the pay station.

From St. Augustine, take SR A1A north for 7 or 8 miles to South Ponte Vedra Beach, then turn left at the signs mentioned above.

Mileage log

0.0   Leave the parking area at the dam, heading west through the

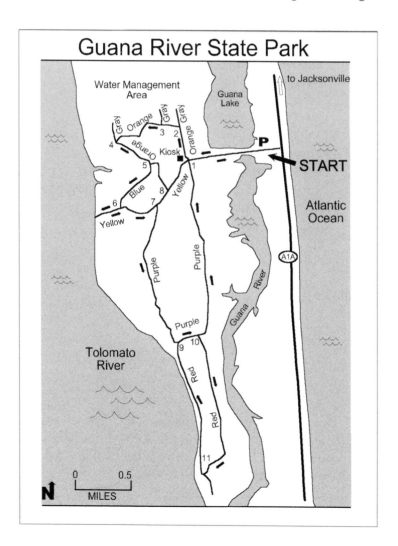

	gate and into the foot-and-bicycle-traffic-only area.
0.3	On your right is a large map of the area you will be riding in, with some photocopied maps you can take with you, and a register to sign in and out on.
0.4	Turn right at marker 1 onto the orange trail.
0.7	Turn left at marker 2 (still on the orange trail). This is a wide single-track.
1.4	Turn left at marker 4 (still on the orange trail). You are back on double-track now.
1.8	Turn right onto the blue trail at marker 5.
2.2	Turn right at marker 6 onto the yellow trail.
2.5	Here, at Shell Bluff, is a nice view of the Tolomato River, part of the Intracoastal Waterway. When you are done here, turn around and head back down the yellow trail the way you came.
2.8	Continue straight on the yellow trail at marker 6.
3.0	At marker 7, turn right onto the purple trail.
4.1	Continue straight on the purple trail at marker 9.
4.2	Turn right onto the red trail at marker 10.
5.6	Turn right at marker 11 (still on the red trail).
6.8	At marker 9, turn right onto the purple trail.
6.9	Turn left at marker 10 (still on the purple trail).
8.3	Turn right onto the yellow trail at marker 1 and head back toward the parking area.
8.7	You are back at the parking area.

For more information, contact:
GTMNERR
505 Guana River Rd
Ponte Vedra Beach, FL 32082
(904) 823-4500

SUWANNEE AREA BIKING

The Suwannee Bicycle Association (SBA) has a wealth of information about so many rides in this area that they cannot be covered in detail in this book. The SBA, in conjunction with the Suwannee River Water Management District and other state government agencies, has developed many miles of off-road trails, some of which are listed below. In addition to these, the SBA also has directions for plenty of nice road rides in the region. For more information, you can contact them at the address at the end of this listing.

Allen Mill Pond Conservation Area provides 4 miles of double-track near an old mill and a spring. The tract is located off CR 251 B, north of Mayo. The entrance is located just before a ninety-degree bend in the road. There is no hunting on this 461-acre tract.

Mattair Springs, on the Suwannee River, has almost 10 miles of riding on old nature trails and fire roads, some of which can be a bit sandy. This area, located northeast of Live Oak, does not allow hunting. You can get to the tract by taking US 129 north from Live Oak, turning east onto CR 136A, turning onto 85th Rd., and then onto 75th Rd., where the entrance is on the left.

Big Shoals State Forest and Conservation Area offers 25 miles of intermediate to challenging riding. In addition to many miles of dirt roads, there are also two single-track trails, the South Trail and the Long Branch Trail. The South Trail winds through the southern part of the tract. The Long Branch trail is a 3- mile single-track loop in the northeast corner. You can get to the tract from US 41 north of White Springs. Turn left onto CR 135, then turn into Big Shoals State Forest. You can park near the Ranger Station. Hunting is allowed in this area, so check with the ranger for hunt dates before riding.

The Little Shoals Tract, a 2.5-mile loop, and **Falling Creek,** approximately 9 miles of looping trails, are in the same area as Big Shoals, but on the other side of the river. Both tracts are part of the Deep Creek Conservation area, adjacent to the Suwannee River. This area does not allow hunting and is located southeast of White Springs. Little Shoals is located off US 41, and Falling Creek is located off CR 246, after turning east from US 41.

Camp Branch Conservation Area offers 6 miles of easy riding on jeep roads and short single-track loops. Located northwest of White Springs, there is no hunting allowed on this tract. It is off of CR 25A, northwest of White Springs, just past I-75 on the west side of the road.

Twin Rivers State Forest, in Ellaville, has 10 miles of easy to intermediate riding on jeep roads and single-track. The single-track portion of this ride is a riverfront trail shared by the Florida Trail, so please be courteous to hikers as you bike this section. In addition, there is a short single-track loop developed by the SBA in the southern portion of the tract. This area can be reached by taking US 90 west from Ellaville. The entrance is on the south side of the road, just west of the agricultural check station.

Contact Information:

Suwannee Bicycle Association
P.O. Box 247
White Springs, FL 32096-0247
(386) 397-2347
Website: http://www.suwanneebike.org
Contact: Kim Frawley, President
woodbike@bellsouth.net
Located in White Springs, a half block north of the intersection of US 41 and SR 136, on Bridge Street

Suwannee River Water Management District
9225 CR 49
Live Oak, FL 32060
(386) 362-1001 or (800) 226-1066 (in Florida)

Big Shoals State Forest
11330 SE County 135
PO Drawer G
White Springs, FL 32096
(386) 397-4331

Twin Rivers State Forest
7620 133rd Rd.
Live Oak, FL 32060
(386) 208-1461

OTHER RIDES IN NORTHEAST FLORIDA

ROAD

The Florida Springs Bicycle Tour is a six-day, 327-mile bicycle tour that visits one national park, ten state parks, and at least ten natural springs. Free maps and directions are available from the Florida Department of Environmental Protection.

Contact:
Florida Department of Environmental Protection,
Office of Greenways and Trails
Mail Station 795
3900 Commonwealth Blvd.
Tallahassee, FL 32399-3000
(850) 245-2052 or (877) 822-5208

Black Creek Trail is an 8-mile paved trail that runs from Orange Park to Black Creek Park north of Green Cove Springs. The trail is shady and passes over several bridges. Use caution, as the trail parallels US 17 and crosses several busy intersections.

Contact:
Florida Department of Transportation
Bicycle/Pedestrian Safety Program
(850) 245-1500

The Suwannee River Greenway is a 25-mile paved trail running from just east of the Suwannee River near Branford to O'Leno State Park in High Springs. The trail is shady and dotted with numerous covered pavilions and benches.

Contact:
Suwannee County Recreation Department
1201 Silas Drive
Live Oak, FL 32064
(386) 362-3004

The Waldo Road Greenway-Depot Avenue Rail Trail is a 6.7-mile trail network running through Gainesville. There are no formal trailheads and it can be accessed at numerous road crossings. Plans are in the works to connect it to the Gainesville-Hawthorne State Trail.

Contact:
City of Gainesville Public Works Department
PO Box 490 MS 58
Gainesville, FL 32602
(352) 334-5074

OFF-ROAD

Cary State Forest, located 25 miles west of Jacksonville, has several miles of fire roads open for hiking. Hunting is allowed in season.
Contact:
Cary State Forest
7465 Pavilion Rd.
Bryceville, FL 32009
(904) 266-5020 or (904) 266-5022

Gold Head Branch State Park, contrary to some popular rumors, has no designated bike trails or single-track at this time. However, bikes are allowed on the 3-mile paved drive. There is an entrance fee (<$5) at the park, which is located 6 miles northeast of Keystone on SR 21.
Contact:
Gold Head Branch State Park
6239 SR 21
Keystone Heights, FL 32656
(352) 473-4701

The Jacksonville-Baldwin Rail Trail is a 14.5-mile paved surface following the course of an old railroad bed. It spans the distance between Baldwin and western Jacksonville. Trailheads are located at both ends. The eastern trailhead is about 1 mile west of I-295, on the west side of Imeson Rd., about 0.5 mile north of its intersection with Commonwealth Ave. The western trailhead is located on the east side of Brandy Branch Rd. (CR 121), a couple of miles west of Baldwin and about 0.3 mile north of US 90.
Contact:
Florida Department of Environmental Protection,
Office of Greenways and Trails
Mail Station 795

3900 Commonwealth Boulevard
Tallahassee, FL 32399-3000
(850) 487-4784

Jennings State Forest's Upper Black Creek Conservation Area has a short hiking trail to a bird-watching site. Hunting is allowed seasonally. The bike trail is located 16 miles southwest of Jacksonville between US 301 and SR 21, off of FL 218. Access is via Nolan Road.

Contact:
Jennings State Forest
1337 Longhorn Rd
Middleburg, FL 32068
(904) 291-5530

O'Leno State Park offers 2 miles of paved road and 13 miles of dirt and sand double- and single-track to riders who are lucky enough to be there when the trails are dry enough to ride. The park trails were too flooded to ride at either of the two times this writer visited the park, though they appeared have great potential when dry. Maps can be obtained at the entrance station, and the ranger will be able to tell you the condition of the trail. The park charges an entrance fee (<$5), and it is located north of Gainesville off US 441.

Contact:
O'Leno State Park
Route 2, Box 1010
High Springs, FL 32643
(386) 454-1853

Osceola National Forest has hundreds of miles of dirt roads open for riding. Hunting is allowed in the forest that is located off of US 90 near Olustee.

Contact:
Osceola National Forest
Osceola Ranger District Office
US Hwy. 90
P.O. Box 70
Olustee, FL 32072
(904) 752-2577

Paynes Prairie State Preserve has an 8-mile loop, 6.5 miles of loop trails, and a 2.6-mile trail for adventurous park visitors. Though some parts of the trail are often damp and others very sandy, these trails can be fun to ride under the right conditions. The trails are mainly easy and flat, offering good opportunities for wildlife viewing. Be sure to check out Chacala Pond, where alligators and birds can often be seen up close. Maps can be obtained at the entrance station. The park, which charges an entrance fee (<$5), is located south of Gainesville on US 441.

Contact:
Paynes Prairie State Preserve
100 Savannah Blvd.
Micanopy, FL 32667
(352) 466-3397

Spirit of the Suwannee is a privately owned park for outdoor recreation, including biking. Six miles of groomed hiking trails are available for riding and are well-suited for family outings. The park has maps of the open trails at the on-site office. There is a small entrance fee. The park is located north of Live Oak off of US 129.

Contact:
Spirit of the Suwannee
3076 95th Dr.
Live Oak, FL 32060
(386) 364-1683

The Stephen Foster State Folk Cultural Center offers a little over 3 miles of off-road biking on flat single-track. The terrain makes this an easy ride, though a little confusing to follow. A map is displayed at the trailhead. The park charges an entrance fee (<$5) and is located off of US 41 in White Springs.

Contact:
Stephen Foster State Folk Cultural Center
P.O. Drawer C
White Springs, FL 32096
(386) 397-2733

Ralph E. Simmons Memorial State Forest allows hiking on Road No. 1 and Road No. 2, 4 to 5 miles in all, on graded forest roads. The parking for these roads is reached by going east on Hampton Rd. from US 1 in Boulogne. Then take a left onto Penny Haddock Rd., and the parking area is on the left.

Contact:
Ralph E. Simmons Memorial State Forest
3472 Clint Dr.
Hillard, FL 32046
(904) 845-3597

BICYCLE CLUBS OF NORTHEAST FLORIDA

Gainesville Cycling Club
5015 NW 19th Pl.
Gainesville, FL 32605
Contact: Chandler Otis
(352) 375-8930 (fax)
Website: www.gainesvillecyclingclub.org
Annual events: Gainesville Cycling Festival, held in October, includes the Horse Farm 100 and Saturn Santa Fe Century rides

North Florida Bicycle Club
P.O. Box 380082
Jacksonville, FL 32205
Contact: Dennis Glasscock, President
dglasscock@comcast.net
Hotline: (904) 721-5870
Website: www.nfbc.com

Suwannee Bicycle Association
Suwannee Bicycle Association
P.O. Box 247
White Springs, FL 32096-0247
(386) 397-2347
Website: http://www.suwanneebike.org
Contact: Kim Frawley, President
E-mail: woodbike@bellsouth.net

Central West

Just one glance at a map will show you that the most prominent features of central west Florida are its coastal cities and towns. The Tampa/St. Petersburg area is centrally located on the coast, and spreading away along the Gulf coast for miles in both directions is an almost seamless progression of development. Where one town ends, the next begins. And it's easy to see why so many people want to live there. The Gulf coast is a beautiful place. Its sun, sand, and water are almost irresistibly attractive. But since most of the population has packed itself in along the coast, most of the good riding is now found, not surprisingly, farther inland, away from the throngs (and thongs) on the beach. This is not to say that there is no good coastal riding in the area-there is quite a bit. In fact, this section includes two very nice Gulf-side rides (see the Longboat Key and Fort De Soto Park rides in the road section). But in general, the farther away from the coast you venture, the more quiet and peaceful the riding gets.

The lay of the land in central west Florida is, as one would expect, quite flat in the coastal areas. Small elevation changes can be found farther inland, but "hilly" is generally not a word used in descriptions of the region's terrain. "Sandy," on the other hand, might tend to pop up now and again when the conversation turns to off-road riding conditions. You knobby-tired riders can rest assured, though, that every effort has been made here, as in the rest of this book, to only include rides that will be doable and pleasurable for most riders.

The weather in central west Florida is great. The area has a relatively low average annual rainfall and fairly moderate temperatures throughout the year. Winters are very subtle, with average lows around 50° F and average highs about 70° F. Summers, of course, are hot, with lows in the mid 70s and highs near 90. And in between, spring and autumn are delightfully temperate. You can be comfortable riding just about any time of the year, but avoiding the heat of the day in the summer months is strongly recommended. Those sultry afternoons are best spent relaxing on the beach or by the pool after having wisely ridden in the cool of the morning.

The cycling scene of the Central West is a thriving one. There are two great rail trails: one urban, the Pinellas Trail; and one rural, the Withlacoochee State Trail. There is a healthy number of off-road riding opportunities and some really good clubs that support them. The Southwest Area Mountain Bike Pedalers (SWAMP), in particular, is a group that anyone interested in off-roading should look up. They build and maintain some really nice trails and organize group rides and annual events. And there are plenty of good road clubs in the region, too. Add to that a fair amount of racing of all varieties, and you have yourself one heck of a lot of fun to be had on two wheels.

ROAD RIDES

LONGBOAT KEY

Location: Sarasota
Distance: 23 miles
Terrain: flat
Description: This out-and-back ride takes advantage of the bike lane along Gulf of Mexico Dr. on the bustling barrier island of Longboat Key. At times, this area can be fairly busy with traffic. This can almost always be a pleasant ride, though, as long as you avoid the high traffic hours, like 5:00 P.M. on weekdays. The scenery is nice and the locals are generally mellow and friendly. Lots of cyclists ride here, so most of the motorists are accustomed and courteous to those on two wheels. The turnaround point for this ride is at Coquina Beach, in Bradenton Beach. However, the more adventurous can continue all the way to the northern tip of Anna Maria Key and see Tampa Bay and the Sunshine Skyway. The going does get more congested, however, and there is no bike lane north of Coquina Beach. This ride can be enjoyed any time of year. Of course, summer afternoons can be quite warm, as there is not much shade along the route. Be sure to drink plenty of water and wear sunscreen.

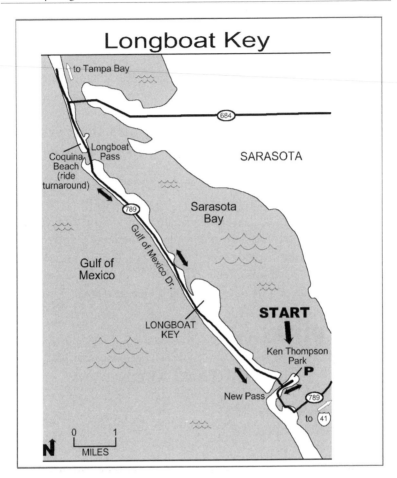

Fees: none

Facilities: There are rest rooms and water at Ken Thompson Park, the starting point. There are also plenty of places to stop along the route.

Finding the ride: From the junction of US 301 and US 41 (Tamiami Tr.) in Sarasota, take US 41 north 1.4 miles and turn left onto John Ringling Blvd. Cross the drawbridge over Sarasota Bay after 1 mile. Continue for 1.3 miles and turn right at St. Armands Circle. Take the first right off of the circle, onto John Ringling Pkwy, and go another 1.1 miles. Turn right onto Ken Thompson Pkwy. at the brown sign for Mote Aquarium. Travel for another 0.4 mile, then turn right at the sign for Ken Thompson Park. You can park on the grass on the left.

Mileage log

0.0	Turn left onto Ken Thompson Pkwy.
0.4	Turn right at the stop sign onto Gulf of Mexico Dr.
0.5	Cross the drawbridge over New Pass. Use caution on the metal grate.
0.6	Enter the Longboat Key city limits.
6.0	Bayfront Park Recreation Center is on your right.
6.1	Enter Manatee County.
8.1	Joan M. Durante Park is on your right.
8.2	There is a bike shop on your right.
10.6	Cross the drawbridge over Longboat Pass. The bike lane ends here.
11.1	Enter the Bradenton Beach city limits.
11.2	Coquina Bayside Park is on your right, with a picnic area, rest rooms, water, a telephone, and a drink machine.
11.5	The Patio Cafe at Coquina Beach is on your left. This is the turnaround point.
11.9	Cross back over the Longboat Pass drawbridge.
16.9	Enter Sarasota County.
22.5	Cross the New Pass drawbridge.
22.6	Turn left onto Ken Thompson Pkwy.
23.0	Turn right, and you are back where you started.

For more information, contact:
Sarasota-Manatee Bike Club, Inc.
P.O. Box 15053
Sarasota, FL 34277-1053
Contact: Tony Renkert, President
(941) 723-5055
Website: http://www.smbc.us
E-mail: info@smbc.us

FORT DE SOTO PARK

Location: St. Petersburg
Distance: 13 miles
Terrain: flat
Description: Fort De Soto Park, in St. Petersburg, is a great place for families, casual riders, and anyone else who wants to ride a bike in pleasant surroundings, unmolested by the heavy automobile traffic that is prevalent in most of the Tampa/St. Pete area. There is a separate, paved bike path paralleling the roadway through much of the park; however, the directions do call for some riding on the park road in places where a separate path is unavailable. Traffic on the road is usually sparse and slow moving. This is a nice place to ride a bike, and there is also plenty of other fun stuff to do.

Fees: <$1 toll to get to the park.

Facilities: There are rest rooms, water, snack bars, picnic areas, swimming, camping, canoeing, and self-guided tours of the fort available at the park.

Finding the ride: From I-275's exit 17 in St. Petersburg, head west on S. 54th Ave. for 2.3 miles. Turn left onto Pinellas Bayway for 4.5 miles until you reach the tollbooth. After the toll, continue straight for 1.2 miles, then turn right at the entrance to the boat ramp area. Follow this road 0.2 mile to the parking lot. The ride starts from there.

Mileage log

0.0	Turn left out of the parking lot, onto the road you came in on.
0.2	Turn right onto Pinellas Bayway at the stop sign.
0.8	At the entrance to the campground, on your right, you can pick up the bike path, which crosses over to the east side of the road in a short distance.
1.8	Straight ahead of you is the park headquarters. Turn right onto Anderson Blvd. at the stop sign.
3.3	The fort is off to your left. There are rest rooms, a gift shop, and a snack bar over there also.
4.3	The bike path crosses over to the east side of the road.
4.6	The bike path ends. Continue straight on Anderson Blvd. Off to your left is the North Beach swim and picnic area. There are rest rooms and a snack bar there.
5.2	Turn around at the cul-de-sac.
5.8	The bike path begins on your left.
6.1	The bike path crosses over to the west side of the road.
7.1	The fort is off to your right.
8.6	Continue straight. (If you have had enough, you can turn left onto Pinellas Bayway and head back to the boat ramp.)
9.6	The bike path ends. Continue straight on the road.
10.1	Here, at the end of the road, is a nice view of Tampa Bay and the Sunshine Skyway. Turn around at the cul-de-sac.
11.6	Turn right onto Pinellas Bayway.
13.2	Turn left at the entrance to the boat ramp area.
13.4	You are back at the parking lot.

For more information, contact:
Fort De Soto Park
3500 Pinellas Bayway S.
Tierra Verde, FL 33715
(727) 582-2267

PINELLAS TRAIL

Location: St. Petersburg/Clearwater/Tarpon Springs
Distance: up to 67 miles
Terrain: flat
Description: The Pinellas Trail has been called a "safe and beautiful asphaltic concrete recreational trail" (asphaltic?), but it is much more than that. It is what very few cities have, but every city needs—and not just one, but lots of them. The Pinellas Trail is a bike and pedestrian path that runs right through the middle of town. It is the perfect way to promote both healthy recreation and clean, quiet, efficient transportation.

The southern end of the trail is in St. Petersburg, and its northern terminus is in charming Tarpon Springs. In between, the trail passes through Seminole, Largo, Clearwater, Dunedin, and Palm Harbor. One of the more pleasurable rides you can do on the trail is to ride from any of these southern points up to Tarpon Springs. Once in downtown Tarpon Springs, follow the signs to the sponge docks and treat yourself to a meal of authentic Greek cuisine at one of the many fine eateries there.

Because it travels through such a developed area, riding this trail is a bit different from riding most of Florida's other trails. You really have to keep your wits about you. There are many street crossings where traffic does not stop for the trail users. Riders must be aware of cross traffic and use due caution. There are also many more users on this trail. It is no place for the speed demon who wants to hammer along nose to stem at warp speed. There are posted speed limits, and they must be obeyed. For further information about the Pinellas Trail, contact the Pinellas County Planning Department. They print a free guidebook that has highly detailed maps and information regarding businesses and public facilities along the trail.

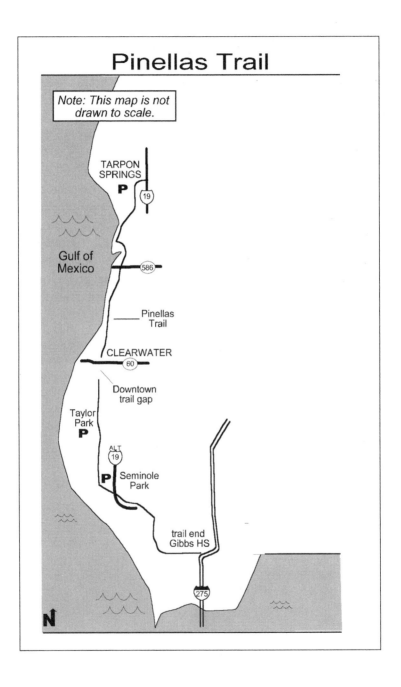

Pinellas Trail

Note: This map is not drawn to scale.

TARPON SPRINGS

P

19

Gulf of Mexico

586

Pinellas Trail

CLEARWATER

60

Downtown trail gap

Taylor Park

P

ALT 19

P Seminole Park

trail end Gibbs HS

275

N

Fees: none

Facilities: Since the trail travels through a mostly urban area, there are plenty of places to find just about any sort of service or facility you might need.

Finding the ride: The Pinellas Trail is easy to find. It crosses just about every major east-west road in Pinellas County. There are plenty of places to leave your car while you use the trail, but here are a couple of the better ones: Seminole Park, at the corner of 74th Ave. and Old Ridge Rd. in Seminole, has rest rooms, water, and picnic facilities. Taylor Park, on the south side of 8th Ave., just west of Ridge Rd. in Largo, has the same amenities plus a reservoir lake. You can also consult the free Guidebook to the Pinellas Trail (see contact information) for specifics on parking and other amenities.

Mileage log: Since there are many possible starting places, and most people will not ride the trail from one end to the other, no specific directions are listed here. Nor are any needed. Just get on the trail and go. Enjoy!

For more information, contact:
Pinellas County Planning Department
600 Cleveland St. Suite 750
Clearwater, FL 33755
(727) 464-8200
or
Pinellas Trails, Inc.
PO Box 356
Clearwater, FL 3357-0356
Website: www.pinellastrails.org
E-mail: pinellastrails@gmail.com

FLATWOODS LOOP

Location: Tampa
Distance: 8 to 21 miles
Terrain: flat
Description: It is not surprising that the paved path at Flatwoods Park is a popular place not only with Tampa area cyclists, but also

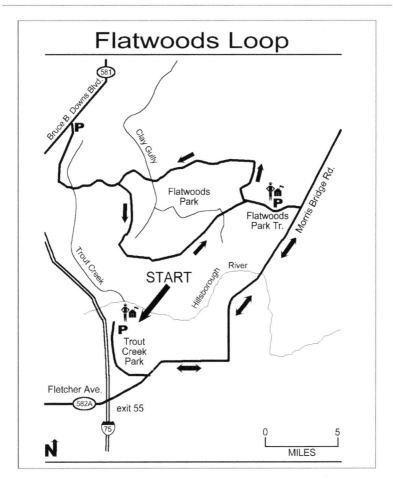

Flatwoods Loop

walkers, runners, and skaters. The path is a 7-mile loop closed to automobile traffic. It is a wonderful place for a peaceful outing: a respite from the noise, stink, and menace of motorized vehicles. Optional directions are included for riding the 6.5 miles from Trout Creek Park to the Flatwoods Loop, which adds 13 miles (out-and-back total) of pleasant road riding to the trip. There is a place on the loop, Clay Gully, that is prone to flooding in the rainy season. Be aware that you may not be able to complete the whole loop when the water is high.

Fees: none

Facilities: There are rest rooms and water available at both Flatwoods Park and Trout Creek Park.

Finding the ride: From I-75's exit 266, head east on Morris Bridge Rd. If you are going to start from Trout Creek Park, turn left after 0.7 mile and follow the park drive 1.5 miles to the parking lot.

Start the ride there. If you want to drive to Flatwoods instead, continue east on Morris Bridge Rd. for another 4.5 miles past the turnoff for Trout Creek Park. Turn left onto Flatwoods Park Trail and go 0.4 mile, then turn right into the parking lot at the entry station. Begin the ride there.

Mileage log
From Trout Creek Park

0.0	Leave the parking lot on the road you came in on.
1.5	Turn left onto Morris Bridge Rd. at the stop sign. There is a bike lane for you to use.
4.6	Cross the bridge over the Hillsborough River.
5.9	Turn left onto Flatwoods Park Trail.
6.5	You are at the entry station. Follow the instructions below to ride the loop.

From the Flatwoods entry station

0.0	Turn right out of the parking lot at the entry station.
0.3	Go straight at the stop sign.
0.6	Turn right at the kiosk and water station, and you are on the loop.
2.9	Clay Gully is the lowest point on the loop. Use caution, since it can be prone to flooding during the rainy season. If you can get across here, you should have no trouble the rest of the way around.
3.5	Stay to the left here to continue around the loop. (Make a right here, and it will take you 2 miles to get to the trailhead at Bruce B. Downs Blvd.)
7.6	You have completed the loop. Go straight to head back to the entry station. (Or turn left if you want to go around again.)
7.9	Go straight at the stop sign.
8.2	Turn left into the parking lot. (Or, if you are riding back to Trout Creek Park, continue straight and go back the way you came.

For more information contact:
Hillsborough County Parks, Recreation
and Conservation Department
1101 East Rivercove St.

Tampa, FL 33604
(813) 975-2160
Website: www.hillsborough county.org/parks

WITHLACOOCHEE STATE TRAIL

Location: Brooksville
Distance: up to 92 miles (46 miles one way)
Terrain: mostly flat

Description: The Withlacoochee State Trail is a great place to ride a bike. Or to skate, walk, run, jog, or ride a horse (on the adjacent bridle path). Part of the Florida Rails-to-Trails Program, the trail makes good use of an abandoned railroad corridor that was formerly going to waste. It is nicely paved, with plenty of room for riding two abreast when the coast is clear (go single file when passing or being passed). You can carry on a conversation, enjoy the scenery, or get lost in your own thoughts without worrying about getting run over by cars, trucks, and RVs. The trail does cross a few roads, however, and you need to be extra careful at these crossings. Riding without having to contend with traffic for extended periods can sometimes desensitize you to the dangers involved. The directions will tell you how to get to

Fun for all on the Withlacoochee State Trail

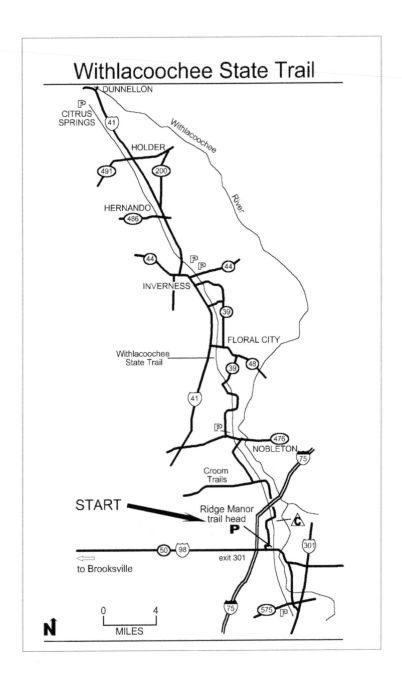

Withlacoochee State Trail

the trailhead near Brooksville, but there are also trailheads near Dunnellon and Inverness. The trail extends southward for 6 miles from the recommended starting point. Be aware that while firearms and hunting are prohibited on the trail, a section of it does pass through the Withlacoochee State Forest, where seasonal hunting is allowed.

Fees: none

Facilities: There are rest rooms and water at the Ridge Manor trailhead.

Finding the ride: From I-75's exit 301, head east on US 98 for 1.4 miles. Turn left at the traffic light onto Croom Rital Rd. and travel for 0.3 mile. Turn right into the trailhead parking lot.

Mileage log: There is no need for instructions to ride this one—you can't get lost. Just turn left onto the trail and ride until you are tired, then turn around and ride back.

For more information, contact:
Withlacoochee State Trail
315 N. Apopka Ave.
Inverness, FL 34450-4201
(352) 726-2251

OFF-ROAD RIDES

BOYETTE

Location: Tampa
Distance: 11 miles
Terrain: easy double-track and moderate single-track
Description: The 5,000-acre Balm Boyette Scrub Preserve is located on and around an old phosphate mining site southeast of Tampa. It contains about 10 miles of double-track trails and 9 miles of single-track. The directions mainly focus on the big single-track loop, which is one of the finest trails to be found in central west Florida. It offers some welcome technical challenges and a real out-in-the-middle-of-nowhere feel. Those looking for something a little simpler will enjoy the double-track's loops around the lakes, and adventurous veterans looking for something that will really test their mettle will want to go check out the berms near the lakes.

Experience the rare, elusive Florida saw palmetto at Boyette.

Fees: none

Facilities: There are no facilities available at the trailhead.

Finding the ride: From exit 246 off of I-75, head east on Big Bend Rd. (CR 672) for 1.5 miles. Make a right turn (south) onto US 301 (still CR 672) and go 1.5 miles. Turn left onto Balm Rd. (still CR 672) for 5.4 miles, then turn left onto Balm Boyette Rd. Travel for 1.3 miles and then turn right into the dirt parking area. That is the trailhead.

Mileage log

0.0	Go around the gate at the end of the parking area and head southeast on the double-track dirt road.
0.2	Turn left into the woods, onto the single-track.
0.9	Make a left, out of the woods, and back onto the double-track.
2.2	Turn right onto the single-track at the bottom of a small gully.
2.4	Cross a double-track.
3.3	Cross another double-track.
4.1	Take the left branch at the fork.
4.4	Stay to the left to continue on the single-track loop. (A right turn here will take you out to the double-track and the berms near the lake.)

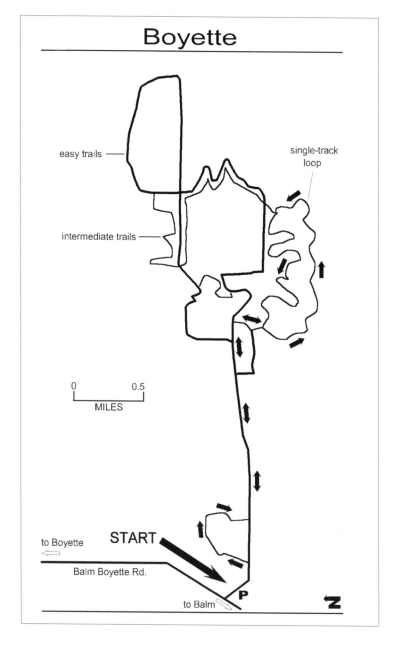

6.8   Turn right onto the double-track, then left onto the single-
       track 50 yards farther.

8.5   Turn right and you are headed back the way you came in.

8.6   Cross a double-track.

| 8.8 | Turn left onto the double-track and follow it back to the trailhead. |
| 11.0 | You are back at the parking area. |

For more information, contact:
Hillsborough County Parks, Recreation
and Conservation Department
1101 East Rivercove St
Tampa, FL 33604
(813) 975-2160
Website: www.hillsboroughcounty.org/parks
or
Southwestern Association of Mountain Bike Pedalers (SWAMP)
1904 Capri Blvd.
Valrico, FL 33594
Contact: Wes Eubank
(813) 988-6435
E-mail: wes@swampclub.org
(813) 689-5109 (hotline)
Website: http://www.swampclub.org

FLATWOODS TO MORRIS BRIDGE

Location: Tampa
Distance: 11-plus miles
Terrain: easy to moderate single-track
Description: Off-road riding opportunities abound in the Lower
Hillsborough Wilderness Park. Within this large park there are three
smaller parks: Flatwoods Park, Morris Bridge Park, and Trout Creek
Park, with trails connecting them. The highlight of the place is the
Morris Bridge Bicycle Area, which is loaded with a maze of single-
track trails. There are some nice trails at Flatwoods, too, where there
is also a paved, 7-mile-long bike path (see the Flatwoods ride in the
road rides of this section). The directions describe how to ride one of
the single-track trails from the Flatwoods Bicycle Area trailhead to the
popular trails at the Morris Bridge Bicycle Area. It is possible to simply
start out at the Morris Bridge Rd. trailhead and get crazy on all of the

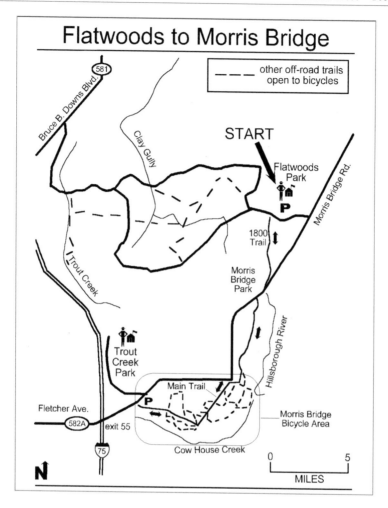

Flatwoods to Morris Bridge

582 581 (Bruce B. Downs Blvd.)

— — — other off-road trails
open to bicycles

Clay Gully

START

Flatwoods
Park

Morris Bridge Rd.

1800
Trail

Morris
Bridge
Park

Trout Creek

Hillsborough River

Trout
Creek
Park

Main Trail

Fletcher Ave.

582A exit 55

75

Morris Bridge
Bicycle Area

Cow House Creek

N

0   5

MILES

single-track there, which many people do. Or, you can warm up or cool down on the paved trail at Flatwoods if you want. So it's your choice. The directions tell you how to get to the Flatwoods trailhead and ride from there to Morris Bridge, but if you prefer to begin at the Morris Bridge trailhead, it is also shown on the map. You will go right by it on your way to Flatwoods. Both Flatwoods and Morris Creek have rest rooms, water, and bike-washing facilities.

However you get there, by car or bike, when you get to the Morris Bridge area you will find a whole mess of trails. Some are well marked and some are not, but the basic setup is that the Main Trail runs right through the middle of the area. It is a wide, easy track blazed with white diamonds that have MAIN TRAIL handwritten on them. It is this trail that this ride is mainly concerned with, but there are many more for you to explore. The Northwestern Trails, which lie to the north and west of the Main Trail, are more challenging. They are blazed in green. The Southeastern Trails, blazed in orange, are found—you guessed it—south and east of the Main Trail. They are also more technical and tend to get a bit soggy in wet weather.

Fees: none

Facilities: There rest rooms, water, and bike washes at Flatwoods and Morris Bridge.

Finding the ride: From I-75's exit 266, head east on Morris Bridge Rd. for 5.2 miles. Turn left onto Flatwoods Park Trail and continue for 0.4 mile. Turn right into the parking lot at the entry station. The ride begins from there.

Mileage log

0.0	Turn right out of the parking lot at the entry station onto the paved road.
0.2	Turn left onto the 1800 Trail at the stop sign.
0.7	Continue straight and ignore the right turn here.
1.2	Ignore the trail off to your left and continue straight.
1.4	A trail merges in from the right.
1.6	Climb up to the guardrail and hop over. Turn right onto Morris Bridge Rd. and cross the bridge over the Hillsborough River.
1.8	Turn left at the first paved drive you come to. Then turn right onto the dirt road.
1.9	Pass by the information station on your right.
2.2	Turn right and go through the gate. You are now entering the Morris Bridge Bicycle Area. There are many side trails here that diverge from the Main Trail. When in doubt of which one is the Main Trail, just follow the path that looks most traveled.
2.9	Cross a small bridge.
3.5	Turn right when you get to the power lines.
3.6	Turn left onto the Main Trail.
3.7	Continue straight to stay on the Main Trail.
4.0	Continue straight to stay on the Main Trail. (A left turn here will take you to the Southeast Trails.)
4.3	Continue straight to stay on the Main Trail. (A left turn here will take you to the Southeast Trails.)

4.4	Turn right to stay on the Main Trail.
4.7	Continue straight to stay on the Main Trail. (A right here will take you to the Northwest Trails.)
5.1	Continue straight at the kiosk to stay on the Main Trail. (A right will take you to the Northwest Trails, and a left turn will take you to the Southeast Trails.)
5.6	You are now at the Morris Bridge Rd. trailhead and have several options. You can: 1) Turn around and go back to Flatwoods the way you came. 2) Turn around and explore some of the other trails here. 3) If you have had enough off-roading, you can turn right onto Morris Bridge Rd. and pound the pavement back to Flatwoods.

For more information, contact:
Hillsborough County Parks, Recreation
and Conservation Department
1101 East Rivercove St
Tampa, FL 33604
(813) 975-2160
Website: www.hillsboroughcounty.org/parks
or
Southwestern Association of Mountain Bike Pedalers (SWAMP)
1904 Capri Blvd.
Valrico, FL 33594
Contact: Wes Eubank
(813) 988-6435
E-mail: wes@swampclub.org
(813) 689-5109 (hotline)
Website: http://www.swampclub.org

CROOM OFF-ROAD BICYCLE TRAIL

Location: Withlacoochee State Forest, Croom Section
Distance: 12 miles
Terrain: moderate single-track
Description: The Croom Section of the Withlacoochee State Forest is the premier off-road riding area in central west Florida. It

has nearly 60 miles of single-track designated for bicycle use. Most of these trails were originally cut by motorcyclists but are now ridden and maintained by the friendly folks of the SWAMP mountain bike club. The instructions below describe how to ride one of the shorter loops known as the Yellow Loop. It's a little sandy in places, but nothing to complain about. It travels through mostly pine forests, with a few modest grades to keep things interesting. And there are plenty more like it for you to explore if you want. The SWAMP group rides the Croom trails regularly. Try giving them a call to see if you can tag along with them on a ride to learn your way around. Caution: There is seasonal hunting in the Withlacoochee State Forest. The trails are closed during muzzle-loading and general gun seasons; call ahead for hunt dates.

Fees: $1 per day parking fee at Tucker Hill Trailhead

Facilities: There is water available at the trailhead.

Finding the ride: From I-75, exit 301 head east on US 98/SR 50 .4 mile. Turn left at the traffic light onto Croom Rital Rd. for 5.6 miles. Take the left branch at the fork, where the name changes to Croom Rd. The pavement ends 0.5 mile past the fork. Go another 3.5 miles and

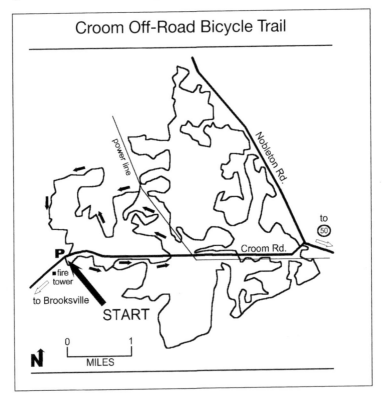

Croom Off-Road Bicycle Trail

park on the left-hand side of the road, just before you get to the fire tower.

Mileage log

0.0	Head into the woods on the single-track marked with bike-trail signs. There is a kiosk with maps and information at the parking lot.
0.1	Take the left branch of this fork.
0.5	Go straight here, over the dirt mound.
0.7	Take the left branch at the fork.
1.2	Go straight at the intersection, staying on the main trail.
1.3	Cross the dirt road (FR 5), then take the left branch at the fork on the single-track.
1.8	Cross under the power lines.
2.5	Cross over to the north side of Croom Rd. and pick up the single-track at the northwest corner of Croom Rd. and FR 7.
2.9	Take the right branch at the fork.
3.4	Cross the hiking trail.
3.6	Take the left branch at the fork.
4.0	The trail turns left and joins a wide track for a short distance.
4.1	Go straight across the blue-blazed horse trail.
4.2	Go straight across the blue-blazed hiking trail.
4.4	As you are going uphill on this wide track, turn left into the woods a short distance after crossing the horse trail again.
5.6	Take the left branch near the top of this hill. (The right branch will take you out to FR 4.)
5.8	Take the right branch at the fork.
6.1	Take the left branch at the fork.
6.2	Take the left branch at the fork.
6.6	Go straight across the dirt road (FR. 5), then take the right branch at the fork. (This is a good bail-out point if you need it. Turn left onto FR 5 for 0.3 mile, then turn right onto Croom Rd. for 0.7 mile and you are back at your car.)
7.8	Turn right onto the double-track.
8.0	Turn left into the woods on the single-track and go straight across the orange-blazed hiking trail.
8.2	Cross the dirt road (FR 4).
8.3	Cross the orange-blazed hiking trail.
9.2	Cross the hiking trail again.
9.6	Go straight across the dirt road.

9.8	Go straight across the dirt road (FR 4).
10.3	Take the left branch at this fork as you are zooming downhill. (The right branch will take you out to FR 3.)
10.5	Take the left branch at the fork.
10.8	Go straight across the dirt road.
10.9	Take the right branch at the fork.
11.2	Take the right branch at the first fork and left branch at the second fork. Then take the right branch at the third fork just after crossing the orange-blazed hiking trail.
11.7	You are back at the parking area near the fire tower.

For more information, contact:
Withlacoochee Forestry Center
Recreation Visitors Center
15003 Broad St.
Brooksville, FL 34601
(352) 754-6896
or
Southwestern Association of Mountain Bike Pedalers (SWAMP)
1904 Capri Blvd.
Valrico, FL 33594
Contact: Wes Eubank
(813) 988-6435
E-mail: wes@swampclub.org
(813) 689-5109 (hotline)
Website: http://www.swampclub.org

OTHER RIDES IN CENTRAL WEST FLORIDA

ROAD

Nature Coast State Trail is a 32-mile paved trail following the course of two old rail lines that meet in Wilcox Junction, connecting the communities of Cross City, Trenton, Fanning Springs, and Chiefland.

Contact:
Florida Greenways and Trails
(352) 555-5181 Monday–Friday
(352) 535-5581 weekends

Suncoast Trail is a 42-mile paved bike path that runs from Tampa through Brooksville, paralleling the Suncoast Parkway toll road.
Contact:
Hillsborough County Parks and Recreation Department
1101 E. Rivercove St.
Tampa, FL 33604
(813) 975-2160

Upper Tampa Bay Trail is a 7.5-mile paved trail that follows an old railroad corridor from Town 'N Country to Citrus Park, passing over Rocky Creek on a wooden suspension trail bridge.
Contact:
Hillsborough County Parks and Recreation Department
1101 E. Rivercove St.
Tampa, FL 33604
(813) 975-2160

Friendship TrailBridge is a 2.6-mile paved trail that connects Tampa and St. Petersburg. The surface of the trail is the deck of the old Gandy Bridge, saved from destruction at the wish of local citizens.
Contact:
Pinellas County Parks Department
631 Chestnut Street
Clearwater, FL 33756
(727) 549-6099

Fred Marquis Pinellas Trail is a 34-mile paved trail connecting St. Petersburg and Tarpon Springs. It connects several parks and communities and passes over numerous scenic bridges. Its multiple parking areas and access points make it a popular choice among cyclists.
Contact:
Pinellas County Planning Department
600 Cleveland St., Suite 750
Clearwater, FL 3375
(727) 464-8201
Venetian Waterway Park contains a new, 9-mile trail running parallel to the Intercoastal Waterway. The Park also contains picnic areas, butterfly gardens, and a fishing dock.

Contact:
Venice Area Beautification, Inc
257 North Tamiami Trail
Venice, FL 34285
(941) 207-8224

OFF-ROAD

Green Swamp and **Green Swamp West** are two water management tracts, located just south of the Richloam tract of the Withlacoochee State Forest. They both offer many miles of riding on dirt roads. While Green Swamp is open for hunting, Green Swamp West is not. The tracts are located off CR 471, just north of US 98. Green Swamp is on the east side of the road, and Green Swamp West is on the west side.

Contact:
Southwest Florida Water Management District
2379 Broad St. (US 41 S.)
Brooksville, FL 34609-6899
(800) 423-1476 or (352) 796-7211, ext. 4470

The Richloam Tract of the Withlacoochee State Forest has 30 miles of double-track to tempt cyclists. You should avoid this area when it is wet, during hunting season, or if you don't want to tackle the occasional sandy spot. From I-75, take exit 301 and head east onto FL 50. Turn south onto CR 471, then turn east onto Claysink Rd. Parking is available near the fish hatchery.

Contact:
Withlacoochee State Forest Visitors Center
15003 Broad St.
Brooksville, FL 34601
(352) 754-6896

Boyd Hill Nature Park, in St. Petersburg, has a 3-mile trail that is open for hiking and biking.

Contact:
Boyd Hill Nature Center
1101 Country Club Way S.
St. Petersburg, FL 33705
(727) 893-7326

Cypress Creek is located near Land O' Lakes and offers 5 miles of paved and unpaved cycling trails. There is no hunting allowed on this tract, which is managed by the Southwest Florida Water Management District. Directions: From US 41 in Land O' Lakes, take CR 583 and follow the CYPRESS CREEK WELLFIELDS signs.

Contact:
Southwest Florida Water Management District
2379 Broad St. (US 41 S.)
Brooksville, FL 34609-6899
(800) 423-1476 or (352) 796-7211, ext. 4470

Flying Eagle allows biking on unpaved woods roads and some horse trails. There are 13 miles of designated shared-use trails in this tract, which does not allow hunting. The tract can be found by taking US 41 north from Floral City and turning right (east) onto Eden Dr. Park at the gate.

Contact:
Southwest Florida Water Management District
2379 Broad St. (US 41 S.)
Brooksville, FL 34609-6899
(800) 423-1476 or (352) 796-7211, ext. 4470

Myakka River State Park has approximately 12 miles of biking on dirt roads. In addition, there are close to 12 miles of horse trails that may be open to cyclists; check with the ranger. The riding area has many hiking trails that are closed to bikes, so when you stop in and pay your entrance fee, pick up a copy of the trail map. This park does not allow hunting. The entrance to the park is on the north side of SR 72, east of Sarasota.

Contact:
Myakka River State Park
13207 SR 72
Sarasota, FL 34241
(941)361-6511
Website: www.myakkariver.org

Jay B. Starkey Wilderness Park, located in New Port Richey, has 6.7 miles of paved multiple-use trails. This area does not allow hunting. From New Port Richey, head west on FL 54. Turn north onto Little Rd. (CR 1) for 1 mile, then go east on River Crossing Blvd. to the park.

Contact:
Pasco County Parks and Recreation Dept.
Central Pasco Professional Ctr.
4111 Land O' Lakes Blvd.
Suite 202
Land O' Lakes, FL 34639-4402
(813) 929-1260

Upper Hillsboro Water Management Area, located near Zephyrhills, 17 miles of woods trails marked for shared-use recreation. This area does allow hunting. From Zephyrhills, head west on FL 54. The entrance is on the south side of the road near the railroad tracks, between FL 54A and CR 35A.

Contact:
Southwest Florida Water Management District
2379 Broad St. (US 41 S.)
Brooksville, FL 34609-6899
(800) 423-1476 or (352) 796-7211, ext. 4470

BICYCLE CLUBS OF CENTRAL WEST FLORIDA

St. Petersburg Cycling Club, Inc.
P.O. Box 76023
St. Petersburg, FL 33734-6023
Website: www.stpetecycling.com
E-mail: goride@stpetecycling.com

Sarasota-Manatee Bike Club, Inc.
P.O. Box 15053
Sarasota, FL 34277-1053
Contact: Tony Renkert, President
(941) 723-5055
Website: www.smbc.us
E-mail: info@smbc.us
Annual events: Gulf Coast Cyclefest, held the first Sunday in November

Suncoast Cycling Club, Inc.

P.O. Box 6112
Palm Harbor, FL 34684-0712
(727) 781-2925
Website: www.suncoasrcycling.com
E-mail: info2006@suncoastcycling.com
Interests: Family-oriented bicycle club offering weekend and weekday rides for cyclists of all levels. Serving mostly mid- and north Pinellas and south Pasco Counties.

Southwestern Association of Mountain Bike Pedalers (SWAMP)

1904 Capri Blvd.
Valrico, FL 33594
Contact: Wes Eubank
(813) 988-6435
E-mail: wes@swampclub.org
(813) 689-5109 (hotline)
Website: http://www.swampclub.org
Annual events: SWAMP Romp, a two-day, fat-tire festival in the Withlacoochee State Forest, Croom Section, is in mid-February; Bike 'n' Brunch, held at Boyette, takes place in early April

Tampa Bay Freewheelers, Inc., bicycle club and TASTE (Tampa and St. Petersburg Tandem Enthusiasts) bicycle group

P.O. Box 1371
Tampa, FL 33601-1371
Contact: Ruben Watson, President
E-mail: rubenwatson@hotmail.com
Website: www.tbfreewheelers.com
Annual events: Strawberry Century, end of March; Free-wheelers Hilly 100, end of September (in conjunction with the St. Petersburg Bicycle Club)

University of South Florida Bike Club

Contact: Quentin McAfee, President
E-mail: qmcafee@hsc.usf.edu
Website: www.ctr.usf.edu/bikes
Interests: road, off-road, racing

Central

When you think of central Florida, do you think of Disney, Sea World, Universal Studios, and Wet 'n' Wild? Well think again, because old Uncle Walt and his disciples don't have anything on what the rest of central Florida has to offer the intrepid cyclist. This region holds some of the best road and off-road riding opportunities the state has to offer. Outside of the larger urban areas of Orlando, Kissimmee, and Ocala there are many miles of quiet country roads and thousands of acres of public land prime for cycling enjoyment.

The Central region ties with the Northwest for the hilliest in the state. Although the Northwest is home to the highest point in the state, central Florida possesses what is widely regarded as the toughest hill climb (see the Sugarloaf Bakery Ride). Don't let an aversion to elevation change scare you away though, because there is also plenty of flatter terrain in the region. Off-roaders will delight in the low sand content of most of the rides in this region.

The winter weather of central Florida is fairly predictable—a bit warmer than in the north and cooler than points farther south. The average winter lows are in the high 40s, and highs are around 70° F. Summers, on the other hand, are some of the warmest in the state. Because central Florida is not privy to the sea breezes that most of the other regions are, things can get quite steamy. Lows are usually in the low 70s, and highs are in the low 90s. Regular summer-afternoon thunderstorms are the saving grace of Central's warm season—they provide welcome relief from the stagnant heat of midday. As in the rest of the state, rainfall tapers off in the cooler months. Average yearly precipitation is around 50 inches.

Due in part, no doubt, to its quantity of excellent riding areas, central Florida has some of the most active and productive cycling communities in the state. There is lots of racing of all kinds. Off-road riding opportunities are steadily expanding. Bike paths and rail-trails are being developed all over the region. And while urban sprawl continues to turn sweet, dreamy country roads into multilane nightmares, it has not yet affected central Florida as badly as it has much of the rest of the state. The region is also home to the Mount Dora Bicycle Festival, the biggest and oldest cycling event in the state. And it has the state's premier off-road riding area (see the Belleview-Santos-Barge Canal-Cross Florida Greenway Off-Road Bicycle Extravaganza). So if it's great riding you are looking for, central Florida's got it. And if it's $3 soda and $5 mouse-shaped ice cream you want, well, that's here, too.

ROAD RIDES

GENERAL JAMES A. VAN FLEET STATE TRAIL

Location: Polk City to Mabel
Distance: up to 58 miles
Terrain: flat
Description: The General James A. Van Fleet State Trail is the most quiet and isolated of all of the Florida rail-trails. It travels 29 miles between Polk City and Mabel, passing through the Green Swamp and crossing the Withlacoochee River along the way. The riding is very peaceful. Most of the time you are surrounded by thick, swampy woods, into which you can see just a short distance because of the dense vegetation. But you can see straight ahead and behind you for miles, because this trail is as flat and straight as they come. There are only a few road crossings, and they are just quiet dirt roads. No matter which end you start from, you can simply ride out as far as you want to go, then turn around and head back.

Fees: none

Facilities: There are rest rooms and water at a small park across the street from the trailhead in Polk City. There are also rest rooms at the Green Pond Rd. access point, 10 miles north of Polk City, and at the Mabel trailhead.

Finding the ride: From I-4's exit 44, take SR 559 north into Polk City. In Polk City, turn left onto SR 33 (Commonwealth Ave.). Exit off of SR 33 where it crosses over SR 655 (Berkely Rd.). The trailhead is

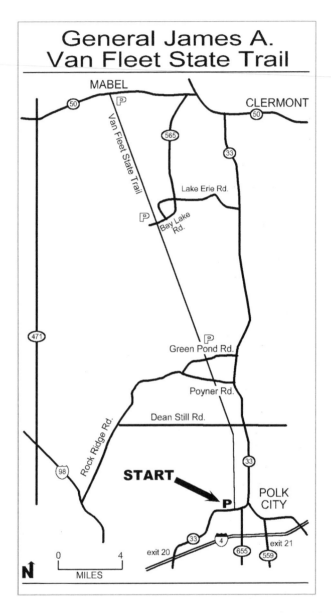

General James A.
Van Fleet State Trail

MABEL

50

CLERMONT
50

Van Fleet State Trail

565

33

Lake Erie Rd.

Bay Lake Rd.

471

Green Pond Rd.

Poyner Rd.

Rock Ridge Rd.

Dean Still Rd.

98

33

START

POLK
CITY

P

33   4

exit 20   655   559   exit 21

0   4

N
MILES

just north of the overpass. Most cyclists will want to start the ride from there, but if you want to find the Mabel trailhead, it is on the south side of SR 50, just east of the bridge over the old railroad corridor.

Mileage log

0.0   Leave the Polk City trailhead and head north on the trail.

5.4	Cross Dean Still Rd.
8.7	Cross Poyner Rd.
9.9	Cross Green Pond Rd. A parking lot and rest rooms are on your right.
20.0	Cross Bay Lake Rd.
29.0	Here is the Mabel trailhead.

For more information, contact:
General James A. Van Fleet State Trail
P.O Box 41
Macotte, FL 34753
(352) 516-7384

SUGARLOAF BAKERY RIDE

Location: Clermont
Distance: 54 miles
Terrain: very hilly
Description: There is some really excellent riding to be found on the roads of Lake County. This area's citrus groves and many lakes provide lush scenery, while the hills supply challenge, speed, and vantage points for some spectacular vistas. This particular ride starts and ends at Clermont Waterfront Park in Clermont and visits a wonderful German bakery in Yalaha. It also includes, on the return trip, a climb over Mount Sugarloaf, widely recognized as the toughest climb in the Sunshine State. At about 310 feet, it is certainly no mountain by anything other than Florida standards, but it is a tough climb nonetheless. Its summit offers a great view of Lake Apopka and the surrounding countryside.

Fees: <$5 parking fee
Facilities: There are rest rooms, water, a playground, and picnic tables at Clermont Waterfront Park.
Finding the ride: From the intersection of US 27 and SR 50 in Clermont, head west on SR 50 for 1 mile. Turn right onto East Ave. and go 0.8 mile. Turn left onto Palm St. and follow it to Clermont Waterfront Park. The ride starts from there.

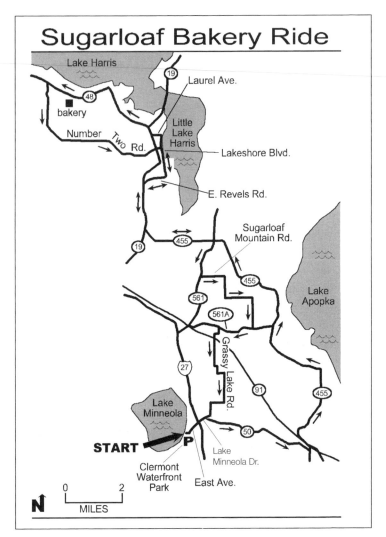

Sugarloaf Bakery Ride

Mileage log

0.0   Get on the bike path by the lake and follow it counter-clock-
wise.

0.3   Follow the path straight across East Ave. Follow the trail to
Mohawk Rd. Take a left on Mohawk and a right on Old Highway 50. Continue east on Old 50.

5.9   At the stop sign, turn left onto CR 455.

6.0   Turn left at the stop sign, staying on CR 455.

8.3   Enter Montverde.

9.4   Turn left at the flashing light, staying on CR 455.

16.8   At the stop sign, go straight across CR 561. It's hard to imagine why anyone would want to, but you can skip the trip to the bakery by turning left onto CR 561 here. Jump down to mile 41.7 and continue following the directions, using the mileages in parentheses. This will shorten the ride by about 25 miles.

19.6   Turn right at the stop sign onto SR 19.

21.3   Turn right onto E. Revels Rd. The name changes to Lakeshore Blvd. at the left curve.

23.7   Turn left onto E. Laurel Ave.

24.0   Turn right onto N. Palm Ave. (SR 19) at the stop sign.

24.4   Continue straight at the traffic light and you will be on CR 48.

27.7   On your left is the Yalaha Country Bakery. You have not yet lived until you have stopped in and sampled some of their yummy baked goods. Turn left onto CR 48 when you have had your fill.

29.1   Turn left onto Number Two Rd.

35.2   Cross SR 19 at the flashing light.

35.3   Turn right onto Lakeshore Blvd.

37.3   Turn left at the stop sign onto SR 19.

38.9   Turn left onto CR 455.

41.7 (16.8)   At the stop sign, turn right (south) onto CR 561.

43.1 (18.2)   Turn left onto Sugarloaf Mountain Rd.

44.2 (19.3)   You are at the top of the climb. There is a nice view of Lake Apopka from here.

46.9 (21.0)   Turn right onto CR 561 A at the stop sign.

48.3 (23.4)   Turn left onto N. Grassy Lake Rd.

49.9 (25.0)   Turn left at the stop sign and stay on Grassy Lake Rd.

For more information contact:
Clermont Parks and Recreation Department
685 W Montrose St.
Clermont, FL 34711
(352) 394-4081 extension 336

MT. DORA SCENIC LOOP

Location: Mt. Dora

Distance: 30 miles

Terrain: moderately hilly

Description: The town of Mt. Dora is a charming place to spend an afternoon or a weekend. The downtown area is loaded with antique shops and restaurants, where one could alternate between browsing and grazing almost indefinitely. The bustling shopping district is surrounded by neighborhoods filled with lovely homes on quiet, shady streets. And, best of all for the cyclist, the surrounding countryside offers many miles of pleasant riding on scenic roads. This particular ride leaves from Donnelly Park in downtown Mt. Dora and returns there after a 30-mile ramble in the country, looping around Lake Dora and Beauclair. Those who find the riding here to their liking might also enjoy the annual Mt. Dora Bicycle Festival. This two-day extravaganza, which takes place the second week of October, is the biggest and longest-running cycling even in the state. It attracts about 1,200 riders each year, offering both road and off-road rides of varying distances and difficulties. Contact the Mt. Dora Chamber of Commerce for more information.

Finding the ride: From the Orlando area, take US 441 north to Mt. Dora. Exit and turn left onto Sanford Rd. (SR 46). Travel 0.8 mile, then turn right onto Highland St. After 0.2 mile, turn left onto 5th Ave. and go another 0.4 mile. Park near Donnelly Park, which will be on your right. The ride leaves from there.

Mileage log

0.0	Leave Donnelly Park, head east on 6th Ave., and cross Baker St.
0.1	At the stop sign, turn right onto Tremain St.
0.6	Follow the left turn in the road. Tremain St. becomes E. Liberty Ave. here.
0.8	Turn right onto Clayton St. at the four-way stop sign.
2.0	At the right turn Clayton St. is now called Beauclair Rd.
2.2	At the left turn Beauclair Rd. becomes Dora Dr.
4.5	Turn right onto Sadler Dr.
5.8	Turn left onto CR 448A at the stop sign.
7.3	Turn right onto CR 48.

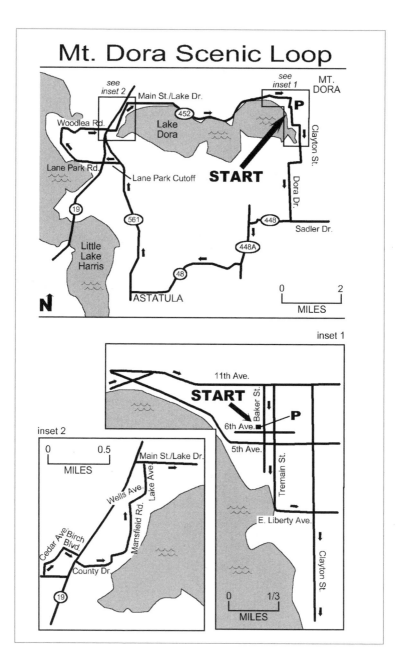

Mt. Dora Scenic Loop

MT. DORA

see inset 2

see inset 1

Main St./Lake Dr.

Woodlea Rd.

452

Lake Dora

P

Clayton St.

Lane Park Rd.

Lane Park Cutoff

START

Dora Dr.

19

561

448

Sadler Dr.

Little Lake Harris

448A

48

0   2
MILES

N

ASTATULA

inset 1

11th Ave.

START

Baker St.

6th Ave.

P

5th Ave.

Tremain St.

inset 2

0   0.5
MILES

Main St./Lake Dr.

Wells Ave.

Lake Ave.

Mansfield Rd.

E. Liberty Ave.

Clayton St.

Cedar Ave.

Birch Blvd.

County Dr.

19

0   1/3
MILES

11.7	Turn right onto Monroe St. (CR 561) at the stop sign.
16.3	Turn left onto Lane Park Cutoff after passing Tavares Middle School on your left.
16.9	Cross US 19 at the flashing red light. (Caution: There is limited sight distance to your right.) The road is now called Lane Park Rd.
19.4	At the right curve the road is called Woodlea Rd.
20.9	Turn left onto Cedar Ave.
21.3	Turn right onto Birch Blvd.
21.4	Turn right onto US 19 (Duncan Dr.) at the stop sign.
21.5	Turn left onto County Dr.
21.6	Take the far left at the five-way intersection.
21.9	Turn right onto Mansfield Rd.
22.4	Turn right onto Wells Ave. at the stop sign.
22.5	Continue straight at the four-way stop sign. The road then curves left and becomes Lake Ave.
22.7	Turn right onto Main St. at the stop sign.
23.5	Go straight at the traffic circle. The road becomes Lake Dora Dr.
23.8	Continue straight at the three-way stop sign. The road becomes Lake Shore Dr. (CR. 452).
28.4	Merge into 11th Ave.
29.1	Turn right onto Baker St.
29.5	You are back at Donnelly Park.

For more information, contact:
Mt. Dora Area Chamber of Commerce
341 N. Alexander St.
Mt. Dora, FL 32757
(352) 383-2165
Website: http://www.mountdora.com
E-mail: chamber@mountdora.com

HORSE FARM FORTY

Location: Ocala
Distance: 40 miles
Terrain: mildly hilly

Description: There is some wonderful riding in the area surrounding Ocala. The rolling green pastures of the region's horse farms supply idyllic scenery, while the hills on the quiet country roads provide a great workout. But while the riding in the outlying areas is spectacular, Ocala proper is decidedly bike *un*friendly. That is why this ride starts at the Paddock Branch of the U.S. Post Office, on the outskirts of town. One could conceivably start in town, but most, if they have access to an automobile, will find driving to the edge of town much more agreeable than cycling there. However you get there, it's a safe bet you will find peaceful, scenic riding once you get into the horse-farm country.

Fees: none

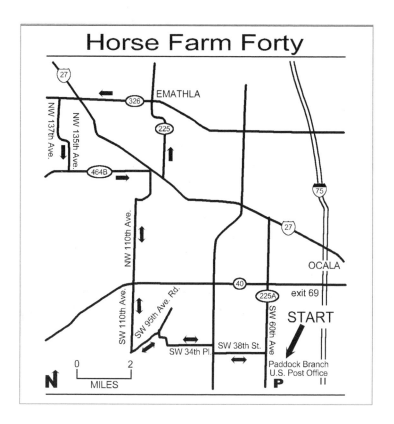

Facilities: There are a couple of convenience stores on the route.

Finding the ride: From I-75's exit 352, head west (away from town) on Silver Springs Blvd. (SR 40). After 2 miles turn left onto SW 60th Ave. (CR 225A) and continue for 3.1 miles. Turn left into the parking lot at the Paddock Branch of the U.S. Post Office. The ride starts from there.

Mileage log

0.0	Turn right out of the post office parking lot onto SW 60th Ave.
0.5	Turn left onto SW 38th St.
2.5	Turn right onto SW 80th Ave. at the stop sign.
2.8	Turn left onto SW 34th Pl.
5.4	Turn left onto SW 95th Ave. Rd. at the stop sign.
6.4	Turn right onto SW 110th Ave.
8.9	Cross SR 40. SW 110th Ave. is now called NW 110th Ave.
13.5	Turn right onto CR 464B at the stop sign.
13.6	Turn right onto US 27 at the stop sign. There is a convenience store here.
14.1	Turn left onto CR 225.
17.3	Turn left onto CR 326 at the red flashing light.
20.0	Cross US 27. There is a convenience store here.
20.8	Turn left onto NW 137th Ave.
22.4	Follow the left curve onto NW 70th St.
22.7	Follow the right curve onto NW 135th Ave.
23.7	Turn left onto CR 464B at the stop sign.
26.9	Turn right onto NW 110th Ave.
31.5	Cross SR 40. NW 110th Ave. is now SW 110th Ave.
34.0	Turn left onto SW 95th Ave. Rd. at the stop sign.
35.0	Turn right onto SW 34th Pl.
37.6	Turn right onto SW 80th Ave. at the stop sign.
37.9	Turn left onto SW 38th St.
39.9	Turn right onto SW 60th Ave. at the stop sign.
40.4	Turn left into the post office parking lot, and you are done.

OFF-ROAD RIDES

LITTLE-BIG ECON

Location: Little-Big Econ State Forest, 20 miles northeast of Orlando
Distance: 3 miles
Terrain: moderate single-track
Description: This trail is mostly flat, slightly sandy single-track that winds through the palmetto thickets of the Little-Big Econ State Forest. The portion of the trail that parallels the creek rolls up and down a bit, but there are no real hills to speak of. Although there is more than just 3 miles of trail in the area, this ride covers the single-track currently designated for bicycle use. There are presently 10–12 miles of bike trail open.

Fees: none

Facilities: There are no facilities at the trailhead. Try Geneva, 3 miles north.

Little-Big Econ State Forest

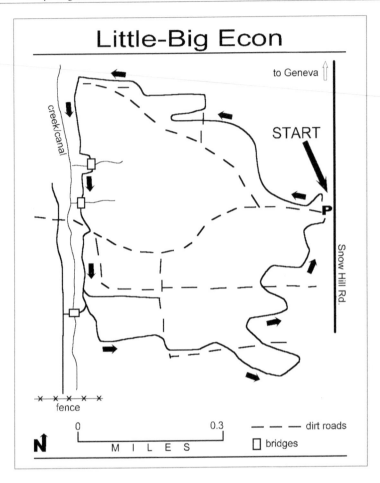

Little-Big Econ

to Geneva

START

P

Snow Hill Rd.

creek/canal

× × × × ×
fence

0   0.3   — — — dir roads
                                 ☐ bridges
N   M I L E S

Finding the Ride: From I-95 exit 223, take SR 46 west for 16.8 miles. Turn left onto SR 426 at Geneva for 0.8 mile. Turn left onto Snow Hill Rd. for 3.4 miles. Turn right into the trailhead parking lot, 0.3 mile after crossing the river.

From Orlando, take SR 426 northeast for about 15 miles. Just south of Geneva, turn right onto Snow Hill Road for 3.4 miles. Turn right into the trailhead parking lot, 0.3 mile after crossing the river.

Mileage Log

0.0   Enter the single-track at the north end of the parking lot (your right as you drove in).

0.9   Turn left here where the single-track meets the double-track.

1.0   The double-track turns left, then narrows down to a single-track.

1.3	Turn left when the single-track reaches the creek.
1.5	Cross a small bridge.
1.6	Cross another small bridge.
1.7	Go straight across the double-track. You can make a side trip off to the right here if you want to get a closer look at the creek.
1.9	Ignore the first single-track off to your left. Turn left onto the second one.
2.0	Turn right when you get to the wide track.
2.2	At this sandy, double-track intersection, make a right turn onto the single-track.
2.5	Cross a double-track.
3.0	Cross another double-track.
3.3	You are at the south end of the parking lot.

For more information, contact:
Little-Big Econ State Forest
Division of Forestry
1350 Snow Hill Rd
Geneva, FL 32732
(407) 971-3500

ROCK SPRINGS RUN STATE RESERVE

Location: 30 miles north of Orlando
Distance: 6 miles
Terrain: easy to moderate single- and double-track
Description: Rock Springs Run State Reserve is a great haven for those who want to take a break from the Magic Kingdom and experience a bit of the animal kingdom instead. Located just 30 miles north of Orlando, it is an easy one-day getaway. The scenery is great, and you are almost sure to see some wildlife along the trail. There are actually two bike trails: the east loop, which is 8 miles long; and the west loop, which this ride covers, is about 6 miles long. The east loop is nice, but the west loop is less sandy and has a bit more single-track. They are both marked with blue blazes and are fairly easy to follow. The scenery is similar on both trails; they roll through mostly pine flatwoods and palmettos. The east loop does have one really cool

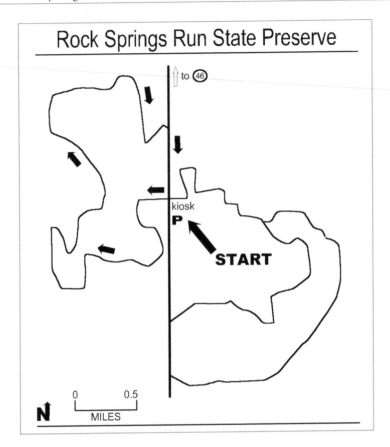

Rock Springs Run State Preserve

to 46

kiosk

P

START

0   0.5

N

MILES

swampy, jungly section, but it doesn't last for long. So, if you only have the time or energy to do one of them, consult the following directions and do the west loop.

Fees: $2 entry fee

Facilities: none available at trailhead

Finding the ride: From west I-4's exit 101BC or East I-4's exit 101C, head west on SR 46 for about 10 miles. The entrance to the preserve will be on your left, 4.5 miles after you cross the Wekiva River. Parking for the bike trailhead is 1.2 miles down the main, paved road, on the left.

Mileage log

0.0	The west loop trail begins across the road from the parking area. Go through the gate and turn left.
0.3	Turn left.

0.4	Turn left onto the sandy double-track.
0.7	Turn right onto the single-track.
1.0	Turn right onto the wide track.
1.4	Turn left onto the sandy double-track.
1.7	Turn right onto the wide single-track.
1.8	Turn right onto the single-track in the palmettos.
2.0	Turn right onto the double-track.
2.3	Turn right.
2.5	Turn right again.
2.6	Turn left.
2.8	Join the horse trail for a short way, then turn onto the single-track.
3.0	Turn right onto the sandy double-track, then turn left onto the single-track again.
3.1	Turn left onto the double track.
3.3	Join the horse trail again.
3.4	Take the left branch at the fork.
3.8	Turn right.
3.9	Turn right onto the single-track.
4.6	Turn right onto the dirt road.
5.3	Turn left onto the wide single-track.
5.5	Turn right onto the pavement.
5.9	You are back at the parking area.

For more information contact:
Wekiwa Springs State Park
1800 Wekiwa Cir
Apopka, FL 32712-2599
(407) 884-2008

PAISLEY WOODS

Location: Ocala National Forest
Distance: 10 to 20 miles
Terrain: easy to moderate single-track
Description: The Paisley Woods Bicycle Trail is a 20-mile loop of single-track that runs between the Alexander Springs Recreation Area

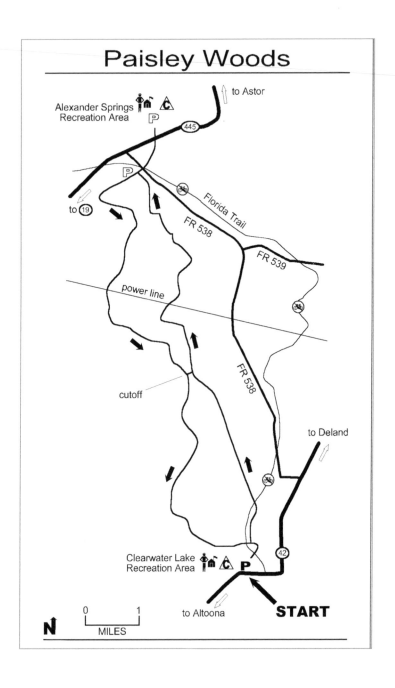

Paisley Woods

Alexander Springs
Recreation Area

to Astor

445

to 19

Florida Trail

FR 538

FR 539

power line

cutoff

FR 538

to Deland

Clearwater Lake
Recreation Area

42

to Altoona

START

N

0   1

MILES

and the Clearwater Lake Recreation Area in the Ocala National Forest. About halfway into the ride there is a cutoff that allows it to be divided into two 10-mile loops. The trail travels through a fairly remote area, offering lots of peace and quiet and plenty of opportunities for wildlife sightings. The terrain is mildly rolling, with the soil fairly sandy. In most places there is enough ground cover to mitigate the sand, but be prepared for some soft footing in spots. The flora varies from shady stands of live oak to piney woods and open wiregrass prairies. The directions for this ride describe how to ride the loop starting from Clearwater Lake, because that trailhead is probably a little easier to get to for most visitors, and it is close to the other facilities of the recreation area. But, if Alexander Springs is more convenient for you, then it is just as good a place to start from. The trail is well-blazed with yellow diamonds, and in places where it makes a pronounced turn, there are half-diamonds turned on their sides to serve as directional arrows.

Fees: none

Facilities: There are rest rooms and water available at both the Clearwater Lake and Alexander Springs Recreation Areas.

Finding the ride: Take SR 19 north from Eustis for about 8 miles. Turn right onto SR 42 at Altoona. After about 6 miles, turn left at the entrance to Clearwater Lake Recreation Area. The trailhead parking is 0.1 mile in, on the right.

Mileage log

0.0	From the Clearwater Lake trailhead parking area, head out on the single-track that starts just to the left of the map kiosk.
0.5	Take the right branch of the fork.
1.2	The bike trail crosses the Florida Trail (hiking only) here.
4.1	Take the right branch of the fork.
4.2	Go straight to continue on to Alexander Springs. (Turn left here, then left again 0.3 mile later if you want to do just the southern loop.)
4.4	Take the left branch at the fork.
4.6	The trail crosses a sandy road, joins a double-track for a short way, then turns left and becomes single-track again.
5.1	Turn left onto the sandy double-track.
5.2	Go straight onto the single-track at the double-track T inter-section.
6.1	Cross under the power lines.

6.2	The trail turns left here.
6.4	Take the left branch of the fork.
6.9	Take the left branch of the fork.
7.2	Turn left at the clearing. Follow the single-track.
7.3	Take the right branch of the fork.
9.0	Turn left here to head back to Clearwater Lake. (To go to Alexander Springs, turn right and follow the single-track 0.9 mile to CR 445. Alexander Springs is on the other side of this road.)
11.3	Turn right onto the sandy double-track.
11.8	Turn left onto the single-track.
11.9	Cross under the power lines.
14.6	Stay to the right at the cutoff.
16.8	Take the left branch at the fork, just after crossing a double-track.
17.7	Turn left onto the double-track.
17.8	Cross a sandy road. The double-track you are on narrows down to a single-track.
18.5	Cross two dirt roads. Follow the wide track along the fence-line on your right.
19.2	Stay to the right at the fork.
19.7	You are back at the Clearwater Lake trailhead.

For more information, contact:
Pittman Visitor Center
45621 SR 19
Altoona, FL 32702
(352) 669-7495
or
Seminole Ranger District
Ocala National Forest
40929 SR 19
Umatilla, FL 32784
(352) 669-3153

THE BELLEVIEW-SANTOS-BARGE CANAL-CROSS FLORIDA GREENWAY OFF-ROAD BICYCLE EXTRAVAGANZA

Location: Ocala
Distance: over 40 miles
Terrain: very easy to very difficult single-track, free-ride area
Description: Back in the 1800s someone came up with the brilliant idea of building a shipping canal across the peninsula of Florida, in order to connect the Gulf of Mexico to the Atlantic Ocean. Land was acquired and work on the project began in the early part of the twentieth century, but for a variety of reasons common sense prevailed and the job was never completed. So the land has now been turned into a 110-mile-long State Recreation and Conservation Area. A decent-sized chunk of it near Santos, south of Ocala, has been designated for mountain-bike trail development. And developed it has been, through the hard work of local enthusiasts with the encouragement of riders throughout the state.

Known by many alternate names, it's officially called the Santos Trailhead Mountain Bike Park. But whatever you want to call it, it is *the* off-road riding destination in the state of Florida. Its 40-plus miles of quality single-track attract mountain bikers the way a pink cycling jersey attracts beer cans on a road ride in redneck country: like a magnet. On any nice weekend, the parking area is full of fun seekers

Fun for all ages at Santos

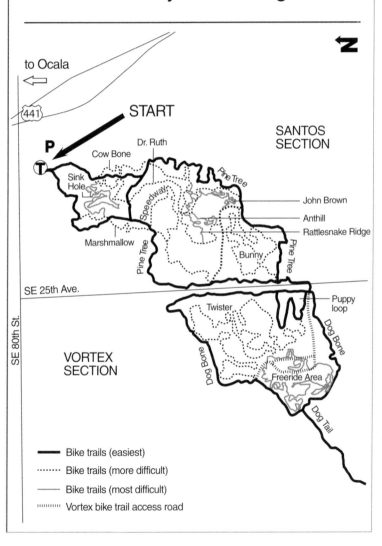

The Belleview-Santos-Barge Canal-Cross Florida Greenway Off-Road Bicycle Extravaganza

tailgating, mingling, posing, polishing, tuning up, and showing off their off-road machines. But the real fun lies in the woods, beyond the social festivities in the parking lot. We are talking single-track galore. There is everything from the simplest wide path to trails that many would find a challenge to walk, let alone ride a bike on, with plenty of everything in between. And there are a couple of fun little playgrounds with tall dirt mounds and steep-sided pits, where daredevil types can frolic and perform trip-to-the-emergency-room-defying stunts. The trails are well-marked as to their names and difficulty levels: Yellow is for easy, blue for moderate, and red for difficult. This place is an example of how a bad idea can sometimes turn into something really great.

Fees: None

Facilities: There are rest rooms at the trailhead and campgrounds.

Finding the Ride: From Ocala, take US 441/301/27 south for about 7 miles. Turn right onto SE 80th St. (CR 328) just past the point where the northbound and southbound lanes diverge and before you get to the Marion County Sheriff's Office. Turn left 0.1 mile later and follow the signs for mountain bike parking.

Mileage Log: One look at the accompanying map will show you why there are no specific instructions here—this trail network is just way too complex for that. Plus, there are so many levels of difficulty that it is impossible to design a ride suitable for everyone. But don't worry. The trails are well marked, and there are usually plenty of riders around to point you in the right direction if you get turned around. And there are usually maps that are larger and more detailed than the one included here available at the kiosk in the parking lot. Be sure to yield to horses at trail crossings!

For more information contact:
Ocala Mountain Bike Association
P.O. Box 2558
Belleview, FL 34221-2558
Contact:Renee Blaney
E-mail: renee.blaney@omba.org
Website: www.omba.org

OTHER RIDES IN CENTRAL FLORIDA

ROAD

The Cady Way Trail, located in the midst of Orlando, is a 3.5-mile paved trail that is used by skaters and pedestrians as well as cyclists. The trail travels from the Fashion Square Mall, near the post office, to Cady Way, near Brookshire Elementary School.

Contact:
City of Orlando
Transportation Planning Bureau
400 S. Orange Ave.
Orlando, FL 32801
(407) 246-2522

The West Orange Trail is a 19-mile paved trail that runs from the western Orange County line east to Apopka. The trail begins just off FL 50 and has a parking area and rest rooms.

Contact:
Orange County Parks and Recreation Department
501 Crown Pointe Cross Rd.
Winter Garden, FL 34787-4845
(407) 654-5144

The Withlacoochee Bay Trail is 5-mile paved trail that runs from Felburn Park near Inglis west to the Gulf of Mexico, travelling through maritime hammocks and salt marshes.

Contact:
Florida Greenways and Trails
(352) 447-1720

The Seminole-Wekiva Trail is a 14-mile paved trail stretching from Altamonte Springs to the Rinehart Road Trail in Lake Mary. The trail follows part of the old Orange Belt Railway, once one of the longest narrow-gauge railways in America.

Contact:
Seminole County Parks and Recreation
264 W. North St.
Altamonte Springs, FL 32714
(407) 788-0405

The Fort Fraser Trail is a new 7-mile trail that runs from SR 540 in Lakeland to SR 60 in Bartow. There are trailheads at Bartow, Highland City, and behind the Polk County Sheriff's Office substation in Lakeland

Contact:

Polk County Leisure Services

(863) 534-4340

The Cross Seminole Trail is a 14-mile paved trail stretching from Orlando's edges to Lake Mary. There are plans to eventually connect the trail with other rail trails such as the Seminole-Wekiva Trail and the Cady Way Trail. The trail is not yet continuous and offers starting points at the Seminole/Orange County line, downtown Oviedo at Railroad Street and North Central Ave., Layer Elementary School in Winter Springs, and paralleling Reinhart Rd. in Lake Mary.

Contact:

Seminole County Trails and Greenways

520 West Lake Mary Blvd, Suite 200

Sanford, FL 32773

(407) 665-2093

Flagler Trail is a new, not-quite-finished trail running from the Orange County line in Chuluota to the St. Johns River north of Lake Harney. Presently, 12 miles of trail running from the Orange County line to the Econlockhatchee River, and from the river to the Geneva Wilderness Area, are open for use. When finished the trail will stretch 18 miles long.

Contact:

Seminole County Parks and Recreation

264 W. North St.

Altamonte Springs, FL 32714

(407) 788-0405

OFF-ROAD

Bull Creek Wildlife Management Area has 15 miles of double-track roads open to bikes. This is a seasonal hunting area managed by the St. Johns River Water Management District. The tract is located 20 miles west of Melbourne on US 192. From US 192, turn south onto

Crabgrass Road. Follow it for 6 miles, where it ends at the entrance station.

Contact:
St. Johns River Water Management District
P.O. Box 1429
Palatka, FL 32178-1429
(386) 329-4500 or (800) 451-7106

The Environmental Studies Center at Soldier Creek has a 3-mile trail on land that is owned by the local school system. The area offers a quick ride close to Orlando, though it is prone to flooding during the rainy season. There are no fees and hunting is not allowed. You can find the Environmental Center by taking FL 419 north from Oviedo. Turn right onto the dirt road and follow the signs to the Environmental Studies Center. You can park near the main building and pick up a map there.

Contact:
Seminole County Environmental Studies Center
2985 Osprey Trail
Longwood, FL 32750
(407) 320-0467

Hal Scott Preserve and Park allows hiking on about 15 miles of trails in an area closed to hunting. To get to the park from Orlando, head east on FL 50, then turn south on FL 520. Turn right onto Maxim Pkwy., then turn left onto Bancroft. Make a right turn onto Meredith and then go left onto Dallas. The park entrance is 1.6 miles down Dallas, on the right.

Contact:
Orange County Parks and Recreation Department
4801 W. Colonial Dr.
Orlando, FL 32808
(407) 836-6200
or
St. Johns River Water Management District
P.O. Box 1429
Palatka, FL 32178-1429
(386) 329-4500 or (800) 451-7106

Highlands Hammock State Park has a 6-mile off-road trail and an 8-mile loop open to bicycles. A short section of it is a paved, tree-lined road, and the rest is dirt. There are bike rentals available, and you can pick up a trail map when you pay your entrance fee at the ranger station. This park does not allow hunting and is located just south of Sebring. From US 27/98, head west on Hammock Rd. (CR 634) to the park entrance.

Contact:
Highlands Hammock State Park
5931 Hammock Rd.
Sebring, FL 33872
(863) 386-6094

Lower Wekiva River State Preserve offers biking on 2.5 miles of nature trails and 18 miles of multi-use trails. This area is subject to flooding, so call ahead to check conditions. To get to the preserve, take exit 101C off I-4 and head west on SR 46. The entrance is on the right, before crossing the Wekiva River. This area does not allow hunting.

Contact:
Lower Wekiva River State Preserve
c/o Wekiwa Springs State Park
1800 Wekiwa Cir.
Apopka, FL 32712
(407) 884-2008

Orlando Wetlands Park/Seminole Ranch Conservation Area offers cyclists 18 miles of berms around wetland cells. The berms are surfaced with ground shells, making for very easy riding. The park is closed from October 1 to January 20 for the hunting season. It is located off of SR 50, northeast of Christmas. Turn north on CR 420, then go right onto Wheeler Rd. (dirt) to the park entrance.

Contact:
Orlando Wetlands Park
25155 Wheeler Rd
Christmas, FL 32709
(407) 568-1706
or
St. Johns River Water Management District
P.O. Box 1429
Palatka, FL 32178-1429
(386) 329-4500 or (800) 451-7106

Prairie Lakes, in the Three Lakes Wildlife Management Area, offers riding on approximately 10 miles of dirt roads. This area is subject to flooding, and hunting is permitted. Prairie Lakes is off of CR 523, approximately 9 miles northwest of Kenansville. Turn west at the entrance to the wildlife management area and park near the check station.

Contact:
Florida Fish and Wildlife Conservation Commission
1329 SW 10th St.
Ocala, FL 34474
(352) 732-1225

Seminole State Forest has over 25 miles of bike-designated roads and trails. Some roads are also used by equestrians, and the forest is open for hunting. From I-4's exit 101C, head west on SR 46. After crossing the Wekiva River, turn onto the first dirt road on the right. Park by the gated entrance and look for a map at the trailhead.

Contact:
Seminole State Forest
9610 CR 44
Leesburg, FL 34788
(352) 360-6675

Tosohatchee State Reserve allows biking on almost 15 miles of service roads, firelines, horse trails, and some hiking trails. All trails marked with white blazes are closed to bicycles and horses. Information and maps can be obtained at the entrance kiosk, where you must pay a small entrance fee. From SR 50 in Christmas, turn south on Taylor Creek Rd. The entrance is on the left, about 3 miles down.

Contact:
Tosohatchee State Reserve
3365 Taylor Creek Rd.
Christmas, FL 32709
(407) 568-5893

Wekiwa Springs State Park has 8 miles of double-track horse trails that are open to bikes as well as a 9-mile long bike trail. A map can be picked up at the entrance station, where you pay your entrance fee. The park does not allow hunting. From exit 94 off of I-4, take SR 434 west. Turn right onto Wekiwa Springs Rd. The park entrance is approximately 4 miles farther, on the right.

Contact:
Wekiwa Springs State Park
1800 Wekiwa Cir.
Apopka, FL 32712
(407) 884-2009

San Felasco Hammock Preserve State Park has 20 miles of off-road single-track trails open to bikes. The terrain is rough, dotted with sinkholes and ravines, so these trails are recommended for more experienced riders.
Contact:
San Felasco Hammock Preserve State Park
12720 NW 109 Ln.
Alachua, FL 32615
(386) 462-7905

BICYCLE CLUBS OF CENTRAL FLORIDA

Florida Freewheelers, Inc.
P.O. Box 916542
Longwood, FL 32791-6524
Contact: George Cheney
E-mail: executivedirector@floridafreewheelers.com
(407) 788-BIKE
Website: www.floridafreewheelers.com

Ocala Mountain Bike Association
P.O. Box 2558
Belleview, FL 34221-2558
Contact: Renee Blaney
E-mail: renee.blaney@omba.org
Website: omba.org

Polk Area Bicycle Association, Inc.
Website: www.polkbiking.com
E-mail: PABAeditor@aol.com
Interests: Touring, weekend rides
Annual events: Bill Carey New Year's Day Century, which takes place on New Year's Day with distances of 25, 65, and 100 miles

Central East

The central east region of Florida is made up of the coastal counties of Volusia, Brevard, Indian River, and St. Lucie, plus the inland Okeechobee County. It is the smallest of the regions in this book, but it has some great places, like Daytona Beach, the John F. Kennedy Space Center, Merritt Island National Wildlife Refuge, and Canaveral National Seashore. And there certainly is no lack of good places to ride a bike. Most notably, there are more than 100 miles of coastal highway inviting road riders to explore the string of barrier islands between Ormond Beach and Ft. Pierce. There is also plenty of nice riding, both on and off-road, to be found on the interior also.

As far as most cyclists will be concerned, there are not many distinguishing geographical features in central east Florida. Those riders that do not like to shift gears very much will be glad to hear that the terrain is mostly flat here. The soil can tend to be on the sandy side in places, but the off-road rides listed in this section are quite manageable. There is not a plethora of options for the off-roader, but those described here are good ones. Also note that some of the trails listed in the central Florida section are within easy day-trip distance of the Central East.

Weatherwise, Central East is about like one would expect. It is a bit warmer than north Florida and a little cooler than south Florida. Winter lows sometimes drop into the high 40s. Average winter highs are in the high 60s, and the overall winter average is in the high 50s. Summer temperatures run from the low 70s to the low 90s, with an average in the low 80s. Yearly rainfall is usually less than 50 inches, which is on the low end of the scale for the Sunshine State. Interestingly, about twice as much rain falls in the warmer months—June, July,

August, and September—than during all the other months of the year, so count on getting wet if you are doing much riding in the summer.

ROAD RIDES

ORMOND BEACH LOOP

Location: Ormond Beach
Distance: 22 miles
Terrain: flat
Description: The northern half of this loop is absolutely gorgeous, with dense canopies over the roadway in places and great scenery along the Halifax River. The southern half is not too shabby, either. It travels

The canopy road at Ormond Beach

Ormond Beach Loop

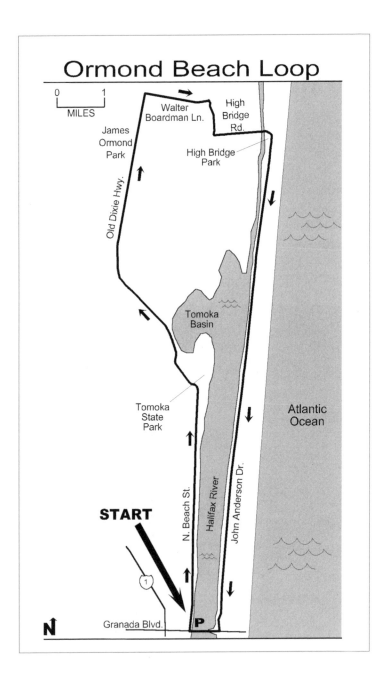

mostly pleasant, residential neighborhood streets. Ormond Bridge, which comes at the end of this ride, can present a bit of a challenge for some, but you can expect to find smooth sailing on level ground the rest of the way around.

Fees: none

Facilities: There are no food stops along the way, but there are plenty of places to find water and rest rooms.

Finding the ride: From I-95's exit 268, head east on Granada Blvd. (SR 40) for 5 miles. Turn left onto N. Beach St., just before the big bridge. Turn right 0.1 mile later, into the parking lot at Riverbridge Gardens Park. The ride leaves from there.

Mileage log

0.0	Turn right out of the parking lot at Riverbridge Gardens Park onto N. Beach St.
3.1	This beautiful section of road is passing through Tomoka State Park.
4.0	Pass the entrance to Tomoka State Park on your right.
4.3	Cross a small bridge. Use caution on the metal grating.
4.7	Stay to the right, on Old Dixie Hwy.
8.6	James Ormond Park is on your left. There are rest rooms and water available there.
9.9	Turn right onto Walter Boardman Ln.
10.9	Cross a small bridge.
11.1	Turn right onto High Bridge Rd.
12.6	Cross the drawbridge over the Halifax River. Use extreme caution on this one, especially if it is wet.
12.7	Pass Highbridge Park, on your right. There are rest rooms and water here.
12.8	Turn right onto John Anderson Dr.
14.6	You are coming back into "civilization" now.
20.0	Go straight at the three-way stop, staying on John Anderson Dr.
21.5	Pass Fortunado Park on your right.
21.6	Turn right at the traffic light onto Granada Blvd. (SR 40) and use the bike lane to cross Ormond Bridge.
22.1	Turn right at the traffic light onto N. Beach St.
22.2	Turn right into the parking lot at Riverbridge Park, and you are done.

For more information, contact:
Daytona Bicycle Club
P.O. Box 731324
Ormond Beach, FL 32173-1324
Website: www.geocities.com/dthigdon/daytonabikeclub

TROPICAL TRAIL TO FAIRYLAND

Location: Melbourne
Distance: 24 miles
Terrain: flat
Description: Tropical Trail (CR 3) is a narrow, shady, two-lane road that runs most of the length of Merritt Island. On its way from Melbourne to Fairyland it travels past stately homes with beautiful yards packed full of tropical-fruit-bearing trees and plants. The riding is easy on this smooth, flat route. It is a pleasure to pedal along while watching boats ply the Intracoastal Waterway on the Indian River. This road has a cozy feeling that is becoming increasingly hard to find in Florida these days.

Fees: none

Facilities: There is water, rest rooms, and a telephone in the Community Services building at Gleason Park, where the ride starts. There are also a pool, picnic tables, shaded pavilions, and a paved path around the lake at Cleason Park.

Finding the ride: In Melbourne, from the intersection of Eau Gallie Blvd. (SR 518) and S. Patrick Dr. (SR 513), just east of the Eau Gallie Cswy., head north on S. Patrick Dr. for 0.5 mile. Turn right at the traffic light, onto Yacht Club Rd. Then take the first right, into the parking lot at W. Lansing Gleason Park, 0.1 mile later.

Mileage log

0.0	Turn left out of the parking lot at Gleason Park onto Yacht Club Blvd.
0.1	Turn right at the traffic light onto S. Patrick Rd. (SR 513).
0.5	Turn left at the traffic light onto Banana River Dr.
0.9	Cross Mathers Bridge (use caution on the metal grating) over to Merritt Island. The road makes a right-hand turn after the

Tropical Trail to Fairyland

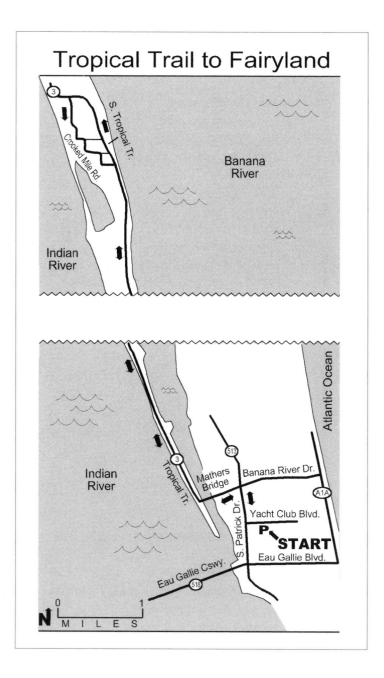

	bridge, and its name changes to Tropical Tr. (CR 3). The body of water on your left is the Indian River.
5.6	Pass underneath SR 404. The body of water you will soon be able to see on your right is the Banana River.
8.2	On your right is a nice little spot to take a rest and look out over the river.
10.4	Turn left onto Crooked Mile Rd.
11.7	Turn right at the stop sign onto S. Tropical Tr. (You can turn left here and go farther north if you want a longer ride.)
11.9	Turn right at the stop sign, staying on S. Tropical Tr.
15.1	There is that rest stop again, now on your left.
18.2	Pass under SR 404 again.
22.9	Be careful crossing back over the drawbridge.
23.3	Turn right at the traffic light onto S. Patrick Dr. (SR 513).
23.6	Just try to ignore that Mister Donut on your left.
23.7	Turn left at the traffic light onto Yacht Club Rd.
23.8	Turn left into the parking lot, and you are finished.

For more information, contact:
Brevard Bike Club
Website: www.geocities.com/bikebbc/

FT. PIERCE TO VERO BEACH VIA
A1A OR VICE VERSA

Location: Ft. Pierce/Vero Beach
Distance: 21 miles
Terrain: flat
Description: This ride takes advantage of the great bike lane that is part of the stretch of A1A between Ft. Pierce and Vero Beach. The route is of the out-and-back variety, with a public park at either end, so this ride may be started from either city. Since each park is right on the beach, an excellent way to end the ride, especially in the summer, is with a dip in the ocean, and maybe a double dip at that ice cream parlor just outside the gates of South Beach Park.
Fees: none
Facilities: There are rest rooms, water, picnic tables, and beach

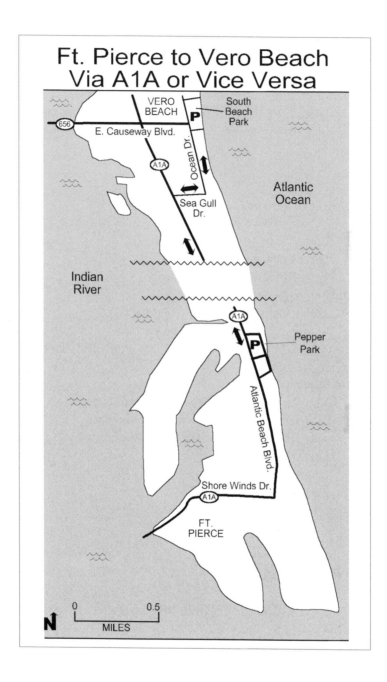

Ft. Pierce to Vero Beach Via A1A or Vice Versa

access available at both parks.

Finding the ride: In Ft. Pierce, go east across the Indian River on North Beach Cswy. (SR A1A N.). Turn left at the traffic light onto Atlantic Beach Blvd. (still SR A1A N.) for 0.7 mile. Turn right into Pepper Park and ride from there.

In Vero Beach, take 17th St. (SR 656) east across the Indian River, where it becomes E. Causeway Blvd. Cross A1A, and 0.3 mile farther go straight at the four-way stop to enter South Beach Park. Park and ride from there.

Mileage log
From Ft. Pierce to Vero Beach

0.0	Turn right onto Atlantic Beach Blvd. (SR A1A) from Pepper Park.
4.4	Enter Indian River County.
9.2	Enter the Vero Beach city limits.
9.8	Turn right onto Sea Gull Dr.
10.0	Turn left onto Ocean Dr.
10.3	There is an ice-cream parlor on your left.
10.4	Turn right at the four-way stop into South Beach Park.

From Vero Beach to Ft. Pierce

0.0	Turn left out of South Beach Park onto Ocean Dr.
0.4	Turn right at the stop sign onto Sea Gull Dr.
0.6	Turn left at the stop sign onto Atlantic Beach Blvd. (SR A1A).
1.2	Leave the Vero Beach city limits.
6.0	Enter St. Lucie County.
10.4	Turn left into Pepper Park.

OFF-ROAD RIDES

SPRUCE CREEK PRESERVE

Location: New Smyrna Beach
Distance: 7 miles
Terrain: moderate single-track
Description: Spruce Creek Preserve offers the best opportunity

Overlooking the oxbow at Spruce Creek

for single-tracking in central east Florida. The riding varies from easy to moderately difficult, as the trails range from wide open to narrow and twisty. There are a few hills. Some of the trails can be a bit sandy in the more open places, but most of them are fairly well shaded and have plenty of ground cover to keep the sand at bay. The bike trails are marked with red and blue. The area is small and not too intimidating to simply ride into and start exploring. The map included here will help you to get the general gist of the place, but be forewarned that there are many side trails and cutoffs that could not be included on the map. Be sure to stay on the existing trails and not make any new ones—there are already more than enough. Also be sure to stop and check out the view of the creek at the bluff overlooking the oxbow; it's a good one.

Fees: none

Facilities: There are no facilities available at the trailhead.

Finding the ride: From New Smyrna Beach, take SR 44 west and turn right onto Sugar Mill Dr., about 0.5 mile before you get to I-95. From I-95's exit 249, take SR 44 east for 0.5 mile and turn left onto Sugar Mill Dr. Follow Sugar Mill Dr. for 1.5 miles, then turn left onto Pioneer Trail for 2 miles. Turn right onto Tumbull Bay Rd for 0.1 mile. Turn left onto the dirt Martins Dairy Rd. Follow it 1.4 miles to the point where it makes a ninety-degree left turn. Park off to the left, just past that turn. The trail starts on the other side of the road at the sign

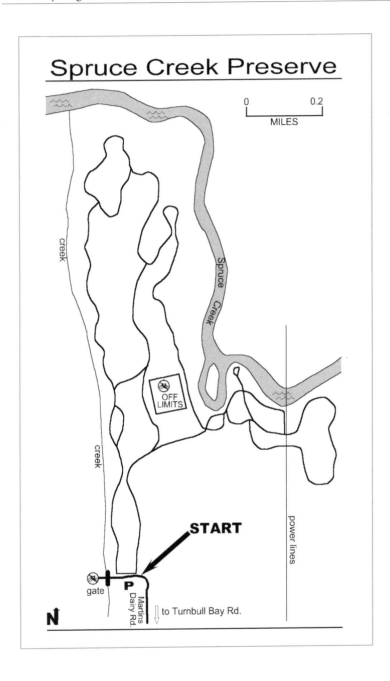

Spruce Creek Preserve

0   0.2
MILES

creek

Spruce Creek

🚲
OFF
LIMITS

creek

power lines

START

🚲
gate

P

Martins
Dairy Rd.

to Turnbull Bay Rd.

N

that reads NO VEHICLES BEYOND THIS POINT.

Mileage log: Because of the intricacy of this trail network, no specific instructions on how to ride it are included here. Just hop on your bike and go have fun. Bring a compass if you are uncomfortable with winging it. For most off-roaders, though, always knowing exactly where you are can spoil the fun.

For more information, contact:
Volusia County Leisure Services
202 N Florida Ave
Deland, FL 32720
(386) 423-3300 extension 5953
Website: www.volusia.org/parks

BLACK POINT WILDLIFE DRIVE

Location: Merritt Island National Wildlife Refuge
Distance: 7 miles
Terrain: flat, graded dirt road

Description: Merritt Island National Wildlife Refuge is a bird watcher's paradise. Black Point Wildlife Drive, within the refuge, offers birders and bikers the best chance to get a close look at some of the 330 species known to alight there from time to time. There are also usually plenty of alligators and other cuddly critters to ogle along the way. The riding on this well-traveled dirt road is easy; it is flat and well packed down in most places. There are some sandy patches, but none terrible enough to stop the average rider on a fat-tired bike. Determined riders on narrower rubber will also do fine. There is not much shade along this route, but summer is not the best time to ride it anyway—the concentration of wildlife is much greater in the fall, winter, and spring. Happily, the biting insect population is smallest at these same times of the year.

Fees: none

Facilities: There are no facilities on the wildlife drive. There are rest rooms, water, and a telephone at the visitors information center on SR 402.

Finding the ride: From Titusville, take the A. Max Brewer Memorial Pkwy. (SR 406/CR 402) east across the Indian River. About 2

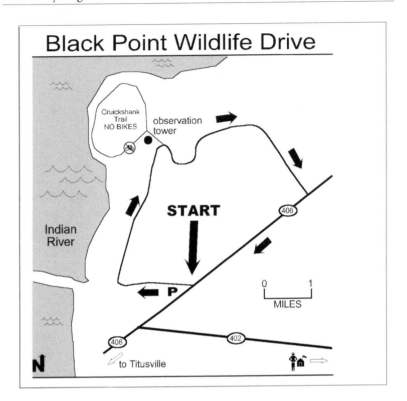

Black Point Wildlife Drive

miles past the bridge, take the left branch of the fork, staying on SR 406. Less than a mile after that, look for the entrance to Black Point Wildlife Drive on your left. You can park on the grass shoulder.

Mileage log

0.0	Enter the wildlife drive.
0.2	There is a place on the left here where you can pick up a guide to the drive.
3.0	Off to your left is a short foot trail (no bikes allowed) leading to an observation tower and the 5-mile Cruickshank Trail (no bikes allowed).
4.9	The road turns to pavement here.
6.0	Turn right at the stop sign onto SR 406.
7.4	You are back at the beginning.

For more information, contact:
Refuge Manager
Merritt Island National Wildlife Refuge
P.O. Box 6504

Titusville, FL 32782-6504
(321) 861-0667
Website: www.fws.gov/merrittisland
E-mail: merrittisland@fws.gov

JACK ISLAND STATE PRESERVE

Location: Ft. Pierce
Distance: 4 miles
Terrain: easy, flat double-track
Description: Jack Island State Preserve offers off-roaders a rare opportunity to cycle through a mangrove estuary. This is made possible by the man-made dike surrounding the swampy mangrove island. The dike, which was made to impound water for the purpose of mosquito control, offers an excellent platform from which to view the abundant plant and wildlife in the mangrove ecosystem. The actual bike riding itself is nothing to rave about to your friends in Colorado, but there are plenty of chances to get up close and personal with animals and plants that you otherwise may never get the chance to experience.

Fees: none

Facilities: There are no facilities at the trailhead. There are rest rooms and water at Pepper Park, 0.2 mile south on A1A.

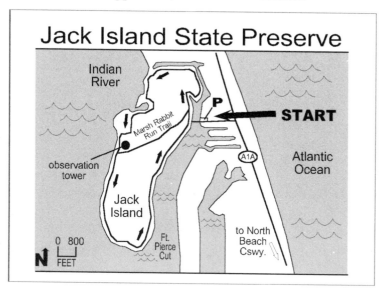

Finding the ride: From Ft. Pierce, go east across the Indian River on North Beach Cswy. (SR A1A N.). Turn left at the traffic light onto Atlantic Beach Blvd. (still SR A1A N.) for 1 mile. Turn left at the brown sign for JACK ISLAND STATE PRESERVE and drive 0.2 mile to the parking area.

Mileage log

0.0	From the parking area, cross the footbridge over to Jack Island.
0.1	Turn right at the kiosk on the other side of the bridge (you can pick up a pamphlet about the trail here) and continue straight past the Marsh Rabbit Run Trail, which goes off to your left.
1.1.	Continue straight here. Off to your left is the dike that bisects the island longitudinally. Then off to your right is an entrance for service vehicles. Continue straight here also.
2.1	Here, on your left, is the observation tower and the other end of the Marsh Rabbit Run Trail. Continue straight.
3.0	Off to your left is the other end of the longitudinal dike.
4.3	You are back at the kiosk. Turn right and go back across the footbridge.
4.4	You are back at the parking area.

For more information, contact:
Ft. Pierce Inlet State Recreation Area
905 Shorewinds Dr.
Ft. Pierce, FL 34949
(772) 468-3985

OTHER RIDES IN CENTRAL EAST FLORIDA

ROAD

The Blue Cypress Water Management Area allows biking on its unimproved levee roads. Located 16 miles northwest of Vero Beach, the area is part of the Blue Cypress Conservation Area, which allows hunting. To park, take SR 60 west from Vero Beach and turn north onto CR 512.

Contact:
St. Johns River Water Management District
P.O. Box 1429
Palatka, FL 32178-1429
(386) 329-4500 or (800) 451-7106
or call the District's Land Management Division at (386) 329-4404

The Lake George Conservation Area is located off US 17, south of Seville. Here you can bike Nine Mile Road to Lake George and a bird-watching area. This is an unpaved road with an out-and-back length of approximately 9 miles. Hunting, fishing, and boating are allowed in this area as well.
Contact:
St. Johns River Water Management District
P.O. Box 1429
Palatka, FL 32178-1429
(386) 329-4500 or (800) 451-7106
or call the District's Land Management Division at (386) 329-4404 or Volusia County at (386) 736-5953

The Lake Woodruff National Wildlife Refuge offers miles of biking on wide dikes surrounding impounded pools on this 19,000-acre tract of land near De Leon Springs.
 Contact:
Lake Woodruff Wildlife Refuge
2045 Mud Lake Rd.
De Leon Springs, FL 32130
(386) 985-4673
Website: www.fws.gov/lakewoodruff

The Ulumay Wildlife Sanctuary has almost 10 miles of single- and double-track located on Merritt Island. At the entrance there is a choice of two trails: the left trail is the longer of the two, and the right trail is shorter, at about 2.5 miles. This area has no maps, no marked trails, and it closes at sunset. The sanctuary is located on the west side of Sykes Creek Rd. between SR 520 and SR 528.
Contact:
Brevard County Parks and Recreation Department
(321) 455-1380

Hontoon Island State Park offers 6 miles of dirt double track roads open to bicycles. Located in the middle of the St. Johns River, the park is reached by a ferry that runs every few minutes.

Contact:
Hontoon Island State Park
2309 River Ridge Rd
DeLand, FL 32720
(386) 736-5309

BICYCLE CLUBS OF CENTRAL EAST FLORIDA

Brevard Bike Club
Website: www.geocities.com/bikebbc

Daytona Bicycle Club
P.O Box 731324
Ormond Beach, FL 32173-1324
Website: www.geocities.com/dthigdon/daytonabikeclub

Spacecoast Freewheelers, Inc.
P.O. Box 320622
Cocoa Beach, FL 32932-0622
(321) 784-4686
Website: www.spacecoastfreewheelers.com
Annual events: Intracoastal Waterways Century, last Sunday in October; Cross Florida Bicycle Ride, 170 miles from Cocoa Beach to Pine Island, first Sunday in May

Southwest

Southwest Florida is probably best known for its resort communities, fine restaurants, and boutique shopping districts, which usually attract visitors who are more interested in golf and tennis than cycling. Hence the proliferation of country clubs, and at first glance, the relative shortage of serious cycling venues. But a closer look will reveal some real gems that the cyclist will relish and even some of the jet-setters may find palatable.

This area of the state is about as flat as they come. The roads are generally straight, sometimes shady (but more often not), and are usually very well-maintained. This makes for fast, easy road riding as long as you stay hydrated. The soil tends to be quite sandy, but there are some places where off-roaders can find firmer footing and easier riding on limestone and gravel roads.

In addition to its sheer beauty, southwest Florida is also blessed with fine weather for enjoying the great outdoors. Winters, of course, are very mild. The locals reach for their warmest winter coats when temperatures drop into the 50s. You should hear them squeal when it plummets to the 40s (which it only rarely does)! Spring and autumn are both very short, but extremely pleasant. Summers are long, hot, and humid, punctuated by brief, but heavy, thunderstorms that appear like clockwork nearly every afternoon. Average summertime temperatures range from the low 70s to the low 90s. Average summer rainfall is a whopping 9 inches per month. Precipitation tapers off dramatically in the cooler months, resulting in an annual average rainfall of around 50 inches.

The cycling scene in southwest Florida is still not quite as vivacious as it is in most of the rest of the state, but it has been steadily improving over the years. The previous lack of off-road opportunities has been rectified by the recent opening of two new trails, one at Caloosahatchee Regional Park, in Lee County, and the other at Collier Seminole State Park, in Collier County. Serious racer types may still not find enough action there to keep them from yearning for greener pastures. Most other riders, however, should be able to find plenty of activity closer to home. It used to be that if you overheard someone in a restaurant mention "cleats" or "links," you could be sure the discussion was about golf. But nowadays, the talk could just be about clipless pedals and bicycle chains. Yes, things are looking really good for bicycling in southwest Florida.

ROAD RIDES

MARCO ISLAND LOOP

Location: Marco Island
Distance: 13 to 22 miles
Terrain: mostly flat
Description: This is a nice loop around the popular vacation destination of Marco Island. It features a roll over Indian Hill, which at 51 feet of elevation, is the highest point in southwest Florida. This "hill" is actually a shell mound, which is believed to have been constructed by the Calusas, ancient inhabitants of the region. The ride also includes an optional trip to the small fishing village of Goodland, where there are a couple of very good seafood restaurants and many interesting characters to chat, drink, or dine with. The riding is easy, on mostly flat, quiet roads. Collier Blvd. and San Marco Dr. can have some fast-moving traffic, but there is generally plenty of room on these roads for everyone.

Fees: <$5 parking fee (free for Collier County residents with a parking permit

Facilities: There are rest rooms, water, beach access, a playground, and a concession stand at Tigertail Beach.

Finding the ride: From SR 951, cross the Marco River Bridge to Marco Island's Collier Blvd. Continue for 1.8 miles, then turn right onto Kendall Dr. After 0.6 mile, turn left onto Hernando Dr. Follow it for 0.2 mile to Tigertail Beach, where you can park and begin the ride.

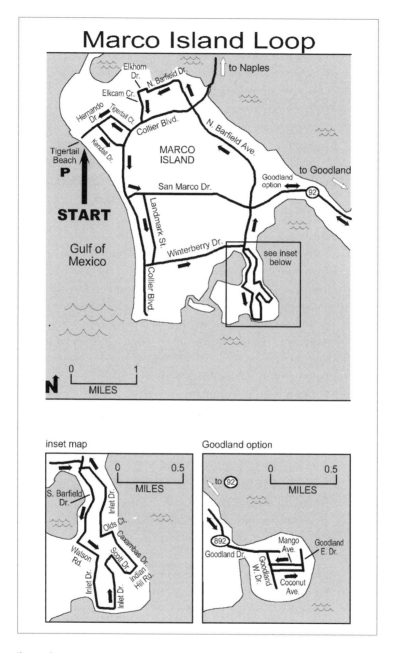

Marco Island Loop

Elkhorn Dr.

to Naples

Elkcam Cr.

N. Barfield Dr.

Hernando Dr.

Tigertail Ct.

Collier Blvd.

N. Barfield Ave.

Tigertail Beach

P

MARCO ISLAND

to Goodland

Goodland option

92

San Marco Dr.

START

Kendall Dr.

Landmark St.

Gulf of Mexico

Winterberry Dr.

see inset below

Collier Blvd

N

0   1

MILES

inset map

0   0.5

MILES

S. Barfield Dr.

Inlet Dr.

Olds Ct.

Caxambas Dr.

Walson Rd.

Scott Dr.

Inlet Dr.

Inlet Dr.

Indian Hill Rd.

Goodland option

0   0.5

MILES

to 92

892

Goodland Dr.

Mango Ave.

Goodland E. Dr.

Goodland W. Dr.

Coconut Ave.

Mileage log

0.0   Exit the parking area and go straight onto Hernando Dr.

0.2   Turn right onto Kendall Dr.

0.8   Turn right onto Collier Blvd. at the stop sign. You can use the

	sidewalk along here if the traffic doesn't look inviting.
1.6	Turn left onto San Marco Dr. at the traffic light.
1.8	Turn right onto Landmark St.
2.9	Turn left onto Winterberry Dr. at the stop sign.
4.4	Turn right onto S. Barfield Dr. at the stop sign.
5.2	Turn left onto Watson Rd.
5.4	Turn right onto Inlet Dr. at the stop sign.
6.3	Turn right onto Scott Dr. at the stop sign.
6.5	Turn left onto Indian Hill Rd.
6.6	You are now at the highest point in southwest Florida.
6.7	Turn left onto Caxambas Dr. at the stop sign.
7.0	Turn left onto Olds Ct.
7.1	Turn right onto Inlet Dr. at the stop sign.
7.8	Turn right onto S. Barfield Dr. at the stop sign.
8.4	Turn right onto San Marco Dr. (SR 29) at the traffic light to head to Goodland. (To bypass the Goodland trip, continue straight here. Jump down to mile 18.8 and follow the directions from there, using the mileages in parentheses.)
11.3	Just before the bridge, turn right onto Goodland Dr. (SR 892).
12.2	Turn right onto Goodland W. Dr.
12.4	Turn left onto Coconut Ave.
12.6	Turn left onto Goodland E. Dr.
12.7	Turn left onto Mango Ave.
12.9	Turn right onto Goodland W. Dr. at the stop sign.
13.0	Turn left onto Goodland Dr. (SR 892) at the stop sign.
13.9	Turn left onto San Marco Dr. (SR 92) at the stop sign.
16.8	Turn right onto N. Barfield Ave. at the traffic light.
18.8 (10.4)	Continue straight across Collier Blvd. at the traffic light.
19.8 (11.4)	Turn right onto Bald Eagle Dr. at the stop sign.
19.9 (11.5)	Turn left onto Elkhorn Dr.
20.0 (11.6)	At the stop sign, turn left onto Elkcam Cir.
20.5 (12.1)	Turn right onto Collier Blvd. at the stop sign. There is also a sidewalk along the road here.
20.8 (12.4)	Turn right onto Tigertail Ct.
21.2 (12.8)	Turn left onto Hernando Dr.
21.7 (13.3)	Go straight at the four-way stop and you are back at Tigertail Beach.

TOUR DI NAPOLI

Location: Naples
Distance: 17 miles
Terrain: flat

Description: This ride passes by miles of million-dollar homes and takes you to some of the most popular attractions in Naples, including the fancy shopping districts on 5th Ave. S. and 3rd. St. S., the beaches, the municipal pier, City Dock, and of course, the fabulous homes of the Port Royal community. The route is mainly comprised of low-traffic streets, but be on the lookout for unalert drivers, especially in the shopping areas and along the beach. Bring your sunscreen, plenty of water, and, if you plan to do any shopping, all the credit cards you can lay your hands on. The ride starts and ends at Lowdermilk Park,

Royal palms along Gordon Drive, Naples

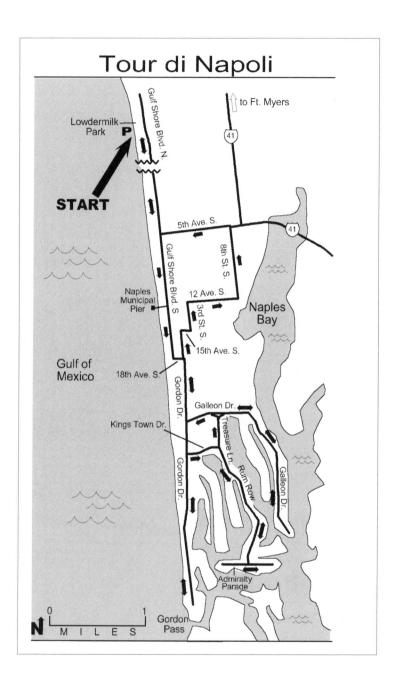

Tour di Napoli

right on the beach, so you also might want to bring your swimsuit and towel.

Fees: <$5 (to park at Lowdermilk Park)

Facilities: There are rest rooms, water, a concession stand, and beach access at the park. There are also a number of places to stop along the way.

Finding the ride: From the Four Corners, the intersection of 5th Ave. S. (US 41/Tamiami Tr. E.) and 9th St. S. (US 41/Tamiami Tr. N.), go west on 5th Ave. S., toward the beach. After 0.8 mile, turn right onto Gulfshore Blvd. S. at the four-way stop. After 1.5 miles, turn left into the Lowdermilk Park entrance, at the traffic light. The ride starts from there.

Mileage log

0.0	Starting from the north end of the parking lot at Lowdermilk Park, turn right onto Gulfshore Blvd. N.
0.1	The entrance to the park is on your right. Continue straight through this traffic light.
1.6	Continue straight at the four-way stop at 5th Ave.S.
2.3	Continue straight at the four-way stop at 12th Ave. S. (A right here will take you to the Naples Municipal Pier.)
2.9	Turn right onto Gordon Dr. at the stop sign.
4.9	Turn around at the cul-de-sac at the end of Gordon Dr.
6.1	Turn right onto Kings Town Dr.
6.6	Take the left branch of the fork, onto Rum Row.
7.6	Turn right onto Admiralty Parade.
7.8	Turn around at the cul-de-sac at the west end of Admiralty Parade.
8.2	Turn around at the cul-de-sac at the east end of Admiralty Parade.
8.5	Turn right onto Rum Row.
9.5	Take the right branch of the fork, onto Kings Town Dr.
9.6	Take the right branch of the fork, onto Treasure Ln.
9.9	Take the right branch at the church, onto Galleon Dr.
10.1	Stay to the left at the fork.
11.3	Turn around at the cul-de-sac at the end of Galleon Dr.
12.4	Stay to the right at the fork.
12.6	Stay to the right and pass the church on your left.
12.9	Turn right onto Gordon Dr. at the stop sign.
13.6	Turn right onto 15th Ave. S.

13.7	Turn left onto 3rd. St. S. at the stop sign. Be careful along here.
14.0	Turn right onto 12th Ave. S.
14.4	Turn left at the traffic circle onto 8th St. S. (going straight here will take you to the City Dock).
15.0	Turn left onto 5th Ave. S. at the traffic light. Be careful along here.
15.7	Turn right onto Gulfshore Blvd. S. at the four-way stop.
17.2	Turn left into Lowdermilk Park at the traffic light, and you are done.

SANIBEL STROLL

Location: Sanibel Island
Distance: 14 to 35 miles
Terrain: flat

Description: The resort community of Sanibel Island is one of the most bike-friendly places in southwest Florida. Since the island is fairly small and the weather is nice all year long, the residents there have had the good sense to recognize that the bicycle is a great means by which to get around in this tropical paradise. Many miles of sidewalks and bike paths exist along the roadways to make hiking as carefree and inviting as possible. This ride starts at Lighthouse Point Park, on the eastern end of Sanibel, and travels some of these bike paths in a loop around the more populated end of the island. For those interested in wildlife viewing, particularly bird-watching, this route will get you out near the J. N. "Ding" Darling National Wildlife Refuge (see the off-road Ding Darling ride in this section). The ride can also be extended up to about a 35-miler by including an out-and-back trip to neighboring Captiva Island. This is an easy, all-season ride that can be enjoyed by anyone interested in salt air, Gulf breezes, and casual cruising among the swaying palms.

Fees: <$5 toll to get onto the island, including parking fee

Facilities: There are rest rooms and water at Lighthouse Point Park. There are also plenty of places to stop for refreshments along the route.

Finding the ride: From Ft. Myers take McGregor Blvd. (SR 867) south and cross the causeway over to Sanibel Island. Continue for 3.5 miles past the tollbooth, then turn left at the four-way stop onto

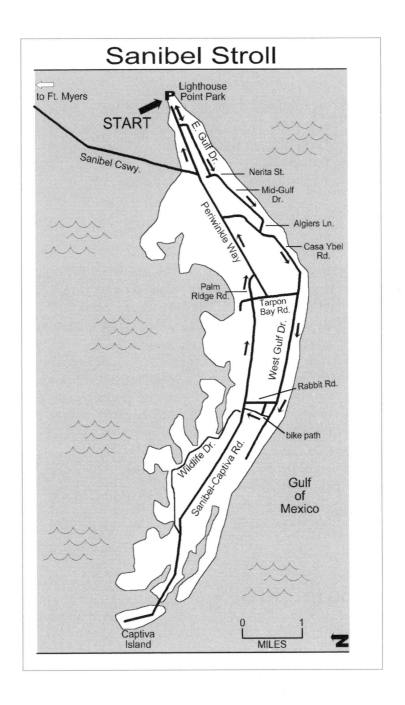

Sanibel Stroll

to Ft. Myers

Lighthouse
Point Park

START

Sanibel Cswy.

E. Gulf Dr.

Nerita St.

Mid-Gulf
Dr.

Algiers Ln.

Casa Ybel
Rd.

Periwinkle Way

Palm
Ridge Rd.

Tarpon
Bay Rd.

West Gulf Dr.

Rabbit Rd.

bike path

Wildlife Dr.

Sanibel-Captiva Rd.

Gulf
of
Mexico

Captiva
Island

0   1
MILES

Periwinkle Way. Go 1.4 miles and continue straight into the entrance to Lighthouse Point Park at the end of Periwinkle Way. The ride starts from there.

Mileage log

0.0	Leave Lighthouse Point Park and head west on Periwinkle Way. There is a bike path that begins just outside the park, on the left-hand side of the road.
0.5	Turn left onto E. Gulf Dr.
2.1	Turn left onto Nerita St. at the stop sign.
2.3	Turn right at the four-way stop onto Middle Gulf Dr.
2.7	Turn right at the four-way stop, remaining on Middle Gulf Dr.
3.7	The bike path crosses over to the other side of the road.
3.8	Stay to the left and follow the bike path through the park.
4.0	The bike path leaves the park and comes out onto Algiers Ln.
4.3	At the stop sign, turn left onto Casa Ybel Rd.
5.1	Continue straight at the four-way stop sign, and you are now on W. Gulf Dr.
7.0	Turn right onto the bike path.
7.9	To head back to Lighthouse Point Park, turn right onto Sanibel-Captiva Rd. (If you are interested in a longer ride, a left turn here will take you 0.3 mile to the entrance to J.N. "Ding" Darling National Wildlife Refuge and 6.6 miles to the Captiva Cswy.
9.7	Continue straight at the four-way stop.
10.0	Turn left onto Periwinkle Way.
12.5	Continue straight at the four-way stop.
13.9	You are back at Lighthouse Point Park.

OFF-ROAD RIDES

BEAR ISLAND

Location: Big Cypress National Preserve
Distance: up to 23 miles
Terrain: easy, flat double-track

Description: This ride, in the Big Cypress National Preserve, will really get you out into the middle of nowhere. And there is no better place than that to see turtles, lizards, alligators, rattlesnakes, wild turkey, quail, and all kinds of wading birds. And although there may still be some lurking around the area, Florida panthers will see, hear, or smell you and skedaddle long before you get a chance to spot them. The route described here is an out-and-back, so you can turn around and go back whenever you are half as tired as you want to be. It travels what is known as the Hardrock Trail, which is a fairly smooth, fast, hard-packed surface. There are many more miles of trail to explore in the preserve, but most of the others tend to be extremely muddy or sandy. The best time to ride this route is in the cooler months; there is little shade, and the biting insects can be quite fierce in the summertime. Note: There is seasonal hunting in Big Cypress National Preserve.

Fees: none

Facilities: Plan to be self-sufficient—there are no facilities nearby.

The nearest basic services are in Immokalee, 20 miles north on SR 29. For anything more extensive (bike shops, hotels, etc.), visit Naples, 30 miles west on I-75.

Finding the ride: From I-75's exit 80, take SR 29 north for 4.3 miles. There will be a gravel road on the right 0.3 mile after crossing a bridge. Park on the shoulder without blocking the gate.

Mileage log

0.0	Use the pedestrian gate, making sure to close it behind you. You are now on the trail.
2.5	There is a pretty pond on the right.
2.8	On your left you can see some of what is left of the cattle company that used to operate here.
3.4	Pass marker 25 on your left.
3.8	Turn left at marker 24.
4.3	Stay to the left at marker 23.
4.8	Pass through the old oil-well area.
4.9	Stay to the left at marker 22.
5.7	Stay to the right at marker 21.
6.1	Continue straight where marker 20 is on your left.
6.2	Stay to the right where marker 18 is on your left.
6.7	Continue straight past marker 17, on your left.
7.3	Continue straight past the campsite, on your right.
7.5	Continue straight past marker 16, on your left.
9.3	Turn left at marker 11.
10.1	Pass the old house on your right.
11.3	Marker 9 signifies the end of the Hardrock Trail. The going gets very muddy beyond here, so this is the turnaround point. Turn around and go back the way you came.
13.3	Turn right at marker 11.
15.3	Continue straight past the campsite, on your left.
16.4	Stay to the left where marker 18 is on your right.
18.3	Stay to the right at marker 23.
18.8	Stay to the right at marker 24.
19.2	Continue straight past marker 25, which is on your right.
22.6	Go back around the gate, and you are done.

For more information contact:
Big Cypress National Preserve
HCR 61, Box 11

Ochopee, FL 33943
(941) 695-4111

DING DARLING

Location: J. N. "Ding" Darling National Wildlife Refuge
Distance: 8 miles
Terrain: wide, flat gravel road
Description: Most people use their cars to drive the 5-mile Wildlife Dr. in the J.N. "Ding" Darling National Wildlife Refuge. That is too bad for them, because sitting in a soundproofed, air-conditioned automobile is no way to experience nature. They may as well just stay home and watch the Discovery Channel. But on your bicycle, you get much more of a sense of what is really going on out there. You have much better visibility. You can feel the warm breezes. You can hear the cries of the osprey, smell the same scents of the wetlands the creatures that live there do, and swat at the same insects that pester them day

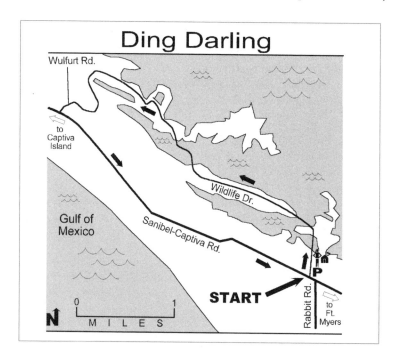

in and day out. There is plenty to see here: all kinds of wading birds and waterfowl, raccoons, alligators, fish—you name it. The road is easy to ride on any mountain bike, cruiser, or hybrid— anything other than a skinny-tired road bike. There are also hiking and canoe trails in the refuge. Bring sunscreen, water, insect repellent, and binoculars. Wildlife Drive is closed to all traffic every Friday.

Fees: $5 entrance fee per car, $6 toll fee

Facilities: There are rest rooms and water available at the visitors center.

Finding the ride: From Ft. Myers, take McGregor Blvd. (SR 867) south and cross the causeway over to Sanibel Island. 3.5 miles past the tollbooth, turn right at the four-way stop onto Periwinkle Way. Continue for 2.5 miles, then take the right branch at the fork, Palm Ridge Rd., for 0.3 mile. Continue straight at the four-way stop and you will then be on Sanibel-Captiva Rd., which will take you 2.1 miles to the refuge entrance, on your right. Park in the lot. Hop on your bike and follow the signs for Wildlife Dr.

Mileage Log

0.0	Enter Wildlife Dr.
1.0	There is a mangrove overlook on your right.
2.0	The observation tower here is worth a visit.
3.9	Turn left onto Wulfurt Rd. at the stop sign.
4.6	Turn left onto Sanibel-Captiva Rd. at the stop sign. There is a separate bike path along here.
7.9	Turn left into the visitors center parking area, and you are done.

For more information contact:
J.N. "Ding" Darling National Wildlife Refuge
1 Wildlife Dr.
Sanibel, FL 33957
(239) 472-1100
Website: www.fws.gov/dingdarling
E-mail: dingdarling@fws.gov

OTHER RIDES IN SOUTHWEST FLORIDA

ROAD

The Gasparilla Island-Boca Grande Trail is a 6.5-mile paved trail running the length of Gasparilla Island. It was the first paved trail built in Florida.

Contact:

Gasparilla Island Conservation and Improvement Association
(941) 964-2667

The Cape Haze Pioneer Trail is a 5.5-mile paved trail that runs from the intersections of SR 776 and SR 771 in McCall to Harness Rd. in Rotunda. Plans are in the works to eventually extend the trail to Placida.

Contact:

Charlotte County Parks and Recreation
4500 Harbor Blvd
Port Charlotte, FL 33952-9175
(941) 627-1628

Oscar Scherer State Park in Osprey offers 2 miles of paved park road and 15 miles of unpaved trails. Pick up a map at the park entrance and remember that there are no restrooms or shelters on the trail.

Contact:

Oscar Scherer State Park
1843 S. Tamiami Trail
Osprey, FL 34229
(941) 483-5956

OFF-ROAD

Caloosahatchee Regional Park, located near Alva, has 10 miles of off-road single track with more being added. The park is open from 8:00 A.M. to dusk year-round. There is a daily parking fee of up to $3. Helmets are required. The park is located between Alva and Ft. Myers on SR 78.

Contact:

Lee County Parks and Recreation

34710 Palm Beach Blvd.
Ft Myers, FL 33916
(239) 461-7400
or Caloosahatchee Regional Park (239) 693-2690

Collier-Seminole State Park has a 3.5-mile, double-track loop for bikers in the Naples/Marco area. Since it is right on the edge of the Everglades, parts of the park are sometimes flooded; the trail is closed at times of high water. If dry, it can be ridden year-round, but the optimum months for riding are December through March. The park is on the south side of US 41, about 10 miles east of SR 951.
Contact:
Collier-Seminole State Park
20200 E. Tamiami Tr.
Naples, FL 34114
(239) 394-3397

Fakahatchee Strand State Preserve, just west of the Big Cypress National Preserve, allows biking on Janes Scenic Dr. This old tram road travels through the preserve for almost 15 miles one way. It is recommended that you not ride past the bridge at the far end of the drive. The preserve is located east of Naples; take US 41 east, turn north onto FL 29, and look for the preserve's entrance on your left.
Contact:
Fakahatchee Strand State Preserve
P.O. Box 548
Copeland, FL 33926
(239) 695-4593

Loop Road Scenic Dr. in Big Cypress National Preserve is 27 miles one way on a one-lane road, most of which is unpaved. The drive loops off of the southern side of US 41. The eastern access point is SR 94, which veers south off of US 41 near the Tamiami Ranger Station. If you continue down this paved section of road, you will pass the Loop Road Environmental Education Center just as the road becomes dirt. You may choose to park there to avoid riding on some of the pavement. The western access point is near Monroe Station. Maps can be picked up at the visitors center on US 41, between Monroe Station and the Tamiami Range Station.

Contact:
Big Cypress National Preserve
33100 Tamiami Trail East
Ochopee, FL 34141
(239) 695-1201

BICYCLE CLUBS OF SOUTHWEST FLORIDA

Caloosa Riders
P.O. Box 870
Fort Myers, FL 33902-0870
Website: www.caloosariders.com
Interests: Road riding
Events: Weekly rides, get-togethers

Coastal Cruisers Bicycle Club
P.O. Box 7424
Port Charlotte, FL 34287-0424
Website: www.coastalcruisers.net
E-mail: webmaster@coastalcruisers.net
Interests: Road, touring, special events
Annual events: Pasta Bash, Saturday in mid-November; 25, 50, and 100 km rides; activities include wine and cheese party, continental breakfast, and then more food; participation limited to 200 riders

Florida Mud Cutters
Contact: Connie Kurash
(239) 561-8581
E-mail: rbag@att.net
Website: www.mudcutters.org

Naples Velo
4051 Skyway Dr.
Naples, FL 34112
Contact: Suzanne Hawkins
(239) 821-3874
E-mail: flyingbig@earthlink.net
Website: www.naplesvelo.org
Interests: Racing

Southeast

Being the most densely populated region of the state, southeast Florida can be, not surprisingly, a very difficult area in which to find nice places to ride your bike. They are there, though. If you are persistent and ask and hunt around, or you are smart enough to purchase a well-written guidebook, you will find them. You will very rarely be completely alone on any of these roads, paths, or trails, as you would often be in north and central Florida. Some people will find that to be a comfort, some find it annoying. Be that as it may, you might lack for solitude, but you will not lack for good riding in southeast Florida.

While this is an area of great ethnic and cultural diversity—you can easily find all kinds of exotic foods to try, and interesting people to ride with—you will be hard-pressed to find much variety in the natural lay of the land. The tallest things around are all creations of mankind: high-rise office buildings and condominiums, concrete road bridges, and rubbish piles (see the Dyer Park off-road ride in this section). Everything else is pretty much dead flat. This generally translates to fast, easy riding for road cyclists. It can mean the same thing for off-roaders too, as long as they choose their routes carefully to minimize the effects of the insidious, speed-sapping sugar sand that is common in this part, and most of the rest of the state.

Weather-wise, things are about what one would expect from a tropical latitude—year-round warmth and humidity with a lot of sunshine and a good bit of rain, too. The summers are hot, but surprisingly no more sweltering than those in most of the rest of the country. The ocean breezes and regular afternoon thunderstorms help to moderate the effects of the sun's intense rays. In fact, the average summer highs in most of southeast Florida are below (albeit barely) 90° F. It is often not the temperature, but the high humidity that makes the summer months uncomfortable for most. The mild winters, of course, are what this area is truly famous for. With lows in the high 50s, highs in the mid 70s, relatively low humidity, and little rain, it is hard to imagine a much more ideal place from which to mail holiday cards to friends and relatives in Minnesota. As mentioned, the summer rains can be significant. July and August often receive up to 9 inches of rain. The cooler months are usually much drier, with averages of only a couple of inches per month.

Not surprisingly, given the great weather and healthy, active population, there is plenty of cycling going on all year long. There are countless clubs and organizations that promote a steady stream of on- and off-road events. Whatever your thing, from short family outings in the park to fast, furious, 40-mile-an-hour sprints on Florida's only velodrome (see the Brian Piccolo Park Velodrome ride in this section), with the help of this guide you will find a place to do it, and plenty of people to do it with, in southeast Florida.

The Keys

You may notice the absence of Florida Keys rides in this section. This is where they would be if there were any, but based on this author's personal experience and interviews with area riders and bike shop employees, there is currently a definite lack of safe, pleasant places to ride a bike for any kind of distance in the Florida Keys. The problem is that there is one main road, US 1, that carries nearly all of the traffic through these islands. Most of US 1 has only two lanes, with many miles of narrow bridges spanning the water between the islands. The heavy flow of trucks, cars, and RVs, often piloted at excessive rates of speed by drivers looking at the scenery instead of the roadway, makes this a rather nasty place for a bike ride. This is not to say that there are not places in the Keys that are good for cycling. Quite the contrary. Key West, for example, is perhaps better traveled and explored by bicycle than by any other means of transport, as is illustrated by the countless places for visitors to rent bicycles. However, providing directions for this kind of riding is difficult. Also, most riders would simply disregard such tedious directions, opting instead to follow their own whims and interests. And well they should, for that is a great part of the appeal of the bicycle in the first place. You can go wherever you want and at your own pace. Those who want someone else to dictate the course of their travels can ride the Conch Train.

Riders yearning for long stretches of open road can take heart in the knowledge that there is a grand plan in the works to build a wide shoulder, and even a separate bike path in places, along US 1 for the entire length of the Keys. The Overseas Heritage Trail, as the path will be known, will eventually stretch 106.5 miles, the entire length of the Keys. Presently the completed, paved section of the path is 61 miles long. Until the trail is completed, those who choose to ride US 1 in the Keys are urged to take the advice of the Florida Department of Transportation: ride only in the early mornings, avoid weekend and holiday riding, and "avoid any possibility of riding during traditional drinking hours (e.g., after 4:00 P.M.)." Yes, by all means, you silly bicyclist, give the drunks some room to enjoy the open road, too. Things are different in the Keys.

ROAD RIDES

JUPITER ISLAND

Location: Jupiter Island, 20 miles north of W. Palm Beach
Distance: 22 miles
Terrain: flat
Description: This out-and-back starts and ends at Jupiter Lighthouse Park. It will take you past miles of stately, elegant homes with well-manicured lawns and yards. This is one of those neighborhoods in which you will see much more of the "hired help"— gardeners, landscapers, pool people, roofers, plumbers, and various other contractors—than the people that actually live there. For some reason, the homeowners are mysteriously absent from the scene. Anyway, let them cloister inside their air-conditioned palaces while you pedal along the shady streets, savoring balmy ocean breezes and drinking in glimpses of the beautiful, deep-blue Atlantic, feeling like the king of the world.
Fees: none
Facilities: There are rest rooms and water at Jupiter Lighthouse Park. There are also rest rooms, water, a telephone, showers, bike racks,

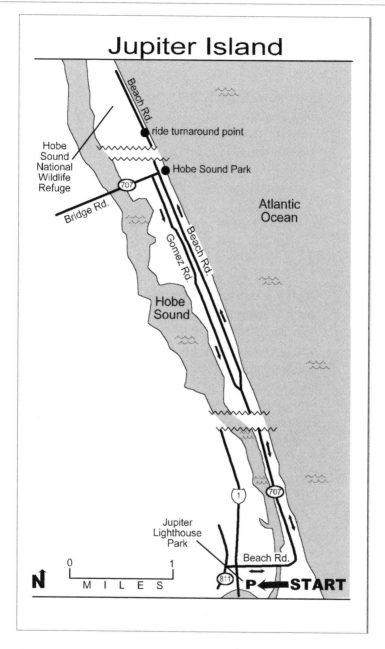

Jupiter Island

ride turnaround point

Hobe Sound National Wildlife Refuge

Hobe Sound Park

Atlantic Ocean

707

Bridge Rd.

Beach Rd.

Gomez Rd.

Hobe Sound

1 707

Jupiter Lighthouse Park

Beach Rd.

0 1

MILES

N

811 P ←START

and beach access at Hobe Sound Park, near the halfway point of the ride.

Finding the ride: From exit 87 off I-95, take SR 706 east for 4.3 miles. Turn left onto US 1. After 1.3 miles, turn right onto Beach Dr.

Take the first right, onto Captain Armours Way, and follow it for 0.3 mile to the parking area near the Lighthouse Visitors Center.

Mileage log

0.0	Leave the parking lot near the Lighthouse Visitors Center on the drive you came in on (Captain Armours Way).
0.3	At the stop sign, turn right onto Beach Rd.
0.6	Cross the drawbridge. Someone at the DOT (who has probably never tried it) recommends that you walk your bike across the bridge.
1.5	Pass Coral Cove Park on your right.
2.0	Enter Martin County and the town of Jupiter Island.
6.9	Take the right branch of the fork.
9.1	Go straight at the stop sign. On your right is Hobe Sound Park, a good place for a rest stop and a swim.
10.8	This is the turnaround point. Directly ahead is the Hobe Sound National Wildlife Refuge, a nice place to enjoy an unspoiled beach.
12.5	Turn right onto Bridge Rd. at the stop sign. This is your last chance to take advantage of the offerings at Hobe Sound Park.
12.	Turn left onto Gomez Rd.
14.8	Go straight at the stop sign, and you are back on Beach Rd.
19.7	Cross back into Palm Beach County.
20.2	Pass Coral Cove Park, your last beach access, on your left.
21.1	Cross the drawbridge. Use caution here.
21.4	Turn left onto Captain Armours Way at the sign for Jupiter Lighthouse Park.
21.7	You are back at the parking lot you started from.

A1A PALM BEACH

Location: Palm Beach
Distance: 25 miles
Terrain: flat
Description: This stretch of SR A1A is a fairly decent one for cycling. In some ways it is similar to the Jupiter Island ride. It takes

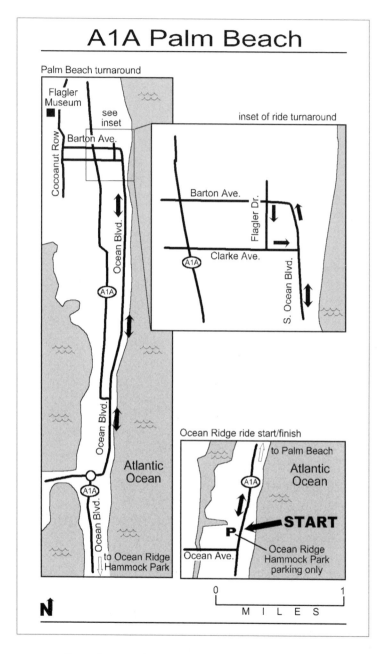

A1A Palm Beach

Palm Beach turnaround

Flagler Museum

see inset

Cocoanut Row

Barton Ave.

Ocean Blvd.

A1A

Ocean Blvd.

Atlantic Ocean

Ocean Blvd.

A1A

Ocean Blvd.

to Ocean Ridge Hammock Park

inset of ride turnaround

Barton Ave.

Flagler Dr.

A1A

Clarke Ave.

S. Ocean Blvd.

Ocean Ridge ride start/finish

to Palm Beach

Atlantic Ocean

A1A

P.

START

Ocean Ave.

Ocean Ridge Hammock Park parking only

0   1
M I L E S

N

you past miles of expensive, expansive homes packed in along the beachfront. The homes here are a bit more ostentatious, sometimes even gaudy. For some reason the residents seem to have an affinity for cement lions, which can be seen flanking the gates and entrances to innumerable homes, making them (in this neighborhood, anyway) more ubiquitous than that infamous Florida lawn decoration, the plastic pink flamingo. But, yard art aside, the scenery is good, the riding is easy, and the sea breezes are pleasant. The traffic will usually be a bit heavier here than on Jupiter Island, but the tradeoff is that this ride is closer and therefore easier to get to from West Palm Beach, Boca Raton, and other points south. The northern extremity of this ride also gets you up in the neighborhood of the Henry M. Flagler Museum, worth a visit if you have not yet been there. From behind the museum you can access a short, 4-mile asphalt trail that runs along Lake Worth and the Intracoastal Waterway up to the northern tip of Palm Beach.

Fees: none

Facilities: There are plenty of public parks with water, rest rooms, and beach access along this route.

Finding the ride: From I-95's exit 57, take Boynton Beach Blvd. east for 0.5 mile. Turn right onto Seacrest Blvd., then take the second left onto Ocean Ave. Follow Ocean Ave. for about 1 mile, until it ends at SR A1A (S. Ocean Blvd.). Turn left onto A1A and after 0.3 mile, turn left again into the small remote parking lot for Ocean Ridge Hammock Park. The ride starts from there.

Mileage log

0.0	Turn left out of Ocean Ridge Hammock Park onto SR A1A (S. Ocean Blvd.).
0.8	Ocean Inlet Park is on your left.
0.9	Cross a small bridge.
3.5	Continue straight through the traffic light at E. Ocean Ave.
4.2	Enter the Palm Beach town limits.
5.5	The Lake Worth Beach and Casino is on your right. There is food, beach access, and a pier there.
5.7	Continue straight through the traffic light at SR 802.
7.3	There is more beach access at Phipps Ocean Park, on your right.
10.0	Enter the traffic circle and take the first right, remaining on A1A/S. Ocean Blvd.
10.7	Continue straight on S. Ocean Blvd. here where A1A turns off to the left.
12.0	The Palm Beach Municipal Beach is on your right.
12.5	The road turns left, and you are now on Barton Ave.
12.6	This is where you turn around and head back south. Turn

left onto Flagler Dr. (If you want to go to the Flagler Museum, go straight here instead and follow Barton Ave. for 0.4 mile. Turn right onto Cocoanut Row and continue for 0.3 mile. The entrance to the museum will be on your left.)

12.8   Turn left onto Clarke Ave.

12.9   Turn right at the stop sign, back onto S. Ocean Blvd.

14.2   This is where A1A joins back in from the right. Continue straight.

14.9   Enter the traffic circle and go three-quarters of the way around, remaining on A1A/S. Ocean Blvd.

19.2   Continue straight at the traffic light at SR 802.

21.4   Continue straight again, at the traffic light at E. Ocean Ave.

24.0   Cross the bridge.

24.9   Turn right into the parking lot at Ocean Ridge Hammock Park, and you are done. If you are ready for a swim now you can walk over to the beach access, just down the street and on the other side of the road.

BOCA TO BOYNTON AND BACK

Location: Boca Raton
Distance: 29 miles
Terrain: flat
Description: This out-and-back ride leaves from South Inlet Park in Boca Raton and travels north on A1A to visit Boynton Beach. The turnaround point is at Ocean Ridge Hammock Park, which is also the starting place for the A1A Palm Beach ride listed in this section. If desired, these two rides can be linked together for an out-and-back totaling 54 miles. Depending on when you ride, you may experience some heavy traffic in the first and last 5 miles of this ride. It should not be too difficult to deal with, however, because the fine people of the city of Boca Raton have provided a nice bike lane to make your journey safer and more pleasant.

Fees: <$10 parking fee at South Inlet Park

Facilities: All of the basic facilities, plus beach access, are available at South Inlet Beach Park. There are also plenty of places to stop for food, drinks, and whatnot along the way.

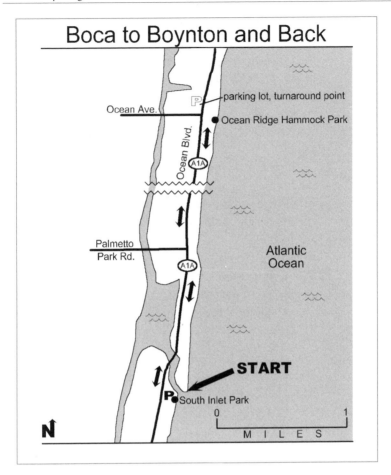

Finding the ride: From I-95, exit 44 in Boca Raton, take Palmetto Park Rd. east. After 3 miles, turn right onto A1A/Ocean Blvd. and continue for 1 mile. Turn left into South Inlet Park just after crossing the drawbridge.

Mileage log

0.0	Turn right out of South Inlet Park onto A1A/Ocean Blvd. There is a bike lane here.
0.1	Use caution crossing the drawbridge. There is no bike lane on the bridge.
4.2	Leave Boca Raton and enter Highland Beach. The bike lane ends here.
9.2	Continue straight at the traffic light at Atlantic Ave. (SR 806).

9.5	On your right is Delray Public Beach, a nice place for a swim.
12.3	On your right is Gulfstream Park, another place to visit the beach.
14.0	Continue straight at the traffic light at Ocean Ave.
14.3	On your left are Boynton Public Beach and Ocean Ridge Hammock Park. This is the turnaround point.
16.3	On your left is Gulfstream Park.
19.1	Here is Delray Public Beach again.
24.4	Enter Boca Raton. The bike path begins.
28.5	Be careful crossing the drawbridge.
28.6	Turn left into South Inlet Park, and you are done.

For more information, contact:
South Inlet Park
1298 S. Ocean Blvd.
Boca Raton, FL 33432
(561) 276-3990 (beach report)
(561) 966-6600 (other information)

THE ROADS OF WESTON

Location: Weston/Sunrise/Davie
Distance: 12 miles
Description: This is a nice training circuit that is convenient to most of the Ft. Lauderdale area. It can be the just right thing for those looking for a fairly safe place to ride without having to first drive many miles. The route travels long, wide, relatively low-traffic, residential neighborhood streets, something of a rarity in this part of the state. There are plenty of other ways to link up the many pleasant streets in this area, but this 12-mile figure eight will get you started. It can be repeated with or without your own variations for a ride of any desired length.

Fees: none

Facilities: Peace Mound Park has a playground, picnic areas, and a nature trail. There are also a few shopping centers nearby, where you should be able to find most of the necessary services and conveniences.

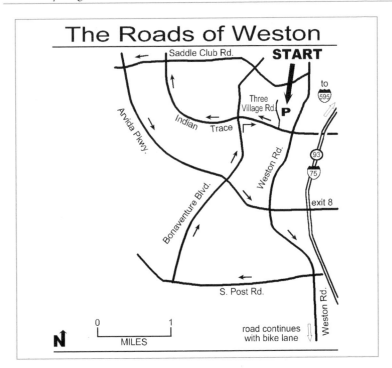

The Roads of Weston

Finding the ride: From Ft. Lauderdale, take I-595 west to exit 1A. From there, take SR 84 west for 2 miles. Turn left at the traffic light onto Weston Rd. (160th Ave.). After 1.6 miles, turn right at the light onto Indian Trace and continue for 0.2 mile. Turn right onto Three Village Rd., travel for 0.1 mile, then make another right into the parking lot at Peace Mound Park. The ride starts from there.

Mileage log

0.0	Turn left out of the parking lot at Peace Mound Park onto Three Village Rd.
0.1	Turn right onto Indian Trace.
0.7	Continue straight at the four-way stop at Bonaventure Blvd.
2.3	At the traffic light, turn left onto Saddle Club Rd.
2.8	Turn left onto Arvida Pkwy. at the four-way stop.
5.1	Continue straight at the four-way stop at Bonaventure Blvd.
5.9	Turn right at the traffic light onto Weston Rd.
7.1	Turn right onto S. Post Rd.
9.1	Turn right onto Bonaventure Blvd. at the four-way stop.
10.8	At the four-way stop at Arvida Pkwy, continue straight.

11.7	Turn right onto Indian Trace at the four-way stop.
12.3	Turn left onto Three Village Rd.
12.4	Turn right, back into the parking lot at Peace Mound Park.

BRIAN PICCOLO PARK VELODROME

Location: Cooper City; 10 miles southwest of Ft. Lauderdale and 15 miles northwest of Miami
Terrain: banked concrete oval track
Description: Those looking to broaden the horizons of their cycling experience should definitely pay a visit to the velodrome at Brian Piccolo Park. With only a handful of such facilities scattered around the country, track riding and racing are elements of the sport of cycling in which few ever get the opportunity to participate. The cyclists of southeast Florida must be proud to boast such a fine venue as the Piccolo Park Velodrome. The park offers track riding classes and regularly scheduled races, which are tremendously exciting to watch.

For the uninitiated, a velodrome is a steeply banked oval track specifically designed for the racing of bicycles. The cycles designed to race on such a track, called track bikes, have one "fixed" gear. A fixed gear is a cog that is rigidly connected, or fixed, to the rear hub. There is no freewheel mechanism. This means that there is no coasting. Whenever the wheel is spinning, the cranks are also spinning. Because

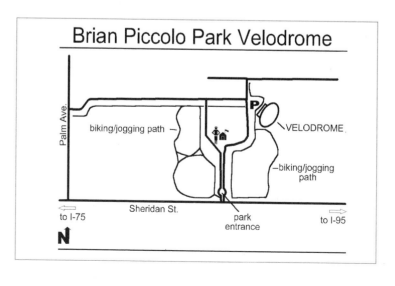

Try riding a track bike on the velodrom at Brian Piccolo Park.

they are intended for racing in close quarters and on a closed course, track bikes do not have any conventional means of braking. They are instead slowed by applying resistance to the turning of the cranks. Track bikes are simple, light, and frighteningly fast. You can rent one at the park and give it a try if you dare.

Fees: <$5 track-use fee, <$10 track-bike rental

Facilities: Rest rooms, water, picnicking, tennis and racquetball courts, a variety of athletic fields, and track-bike rentals are offered at the park.

Finding the ride: From I-95's exit 21, take Sheridan St. west for 6.5 miles and turn right into the park entrance. Travel 0.1 mile past the gatehouse, then turn right. The velodrome parking is about 0.2 mile farther, on the right.

For more information, contact:
Brian Piccolo Park
9501 Sheridan St.
Cooper City, FL 33024
Park office: (954) 437-2600; Velodrome: (954) 437-2626

COCONUT GROVE TO KEY BISCAYNE

Location: Miami
Distance: 22 miles
Terrain: flat
Description: Perhaps the most popular, and surely one of the nicest road rides in the Miami area, this route takes advantage of the separate bike path along the Rickenbacker Cswy. out to Virginia Key and Key Biscayne. It leaves from Peacock Park, in funky Coconut Grove. There are plenty of places nearby for food and drink either before or after the ride. The route will take you past Vizcaya Museum and Gardens, the Miami Seaquarium, and the Bill Baggs Cape Florida State Recreation Area. Bring your sunglasses, wear sunscreen, and,

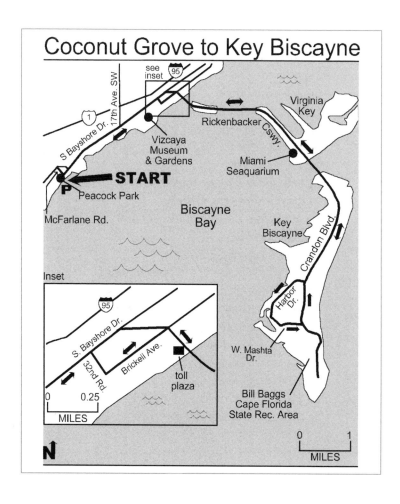

since the scenery along the bike path is usually very nice, remember to keep one eye on the road.

Fees: <$5 parking fee

Facilities: There are rest rooms and water available at the park, and just about anything else you could want is nearby.

Finding the ride: From Miami and points north, take I-95 south past exit 1, where it becomes US 1/S. Dixie Hwy. Turn left onto SW 17th Ave. After 0.6 mile, turn right onto S. Bayshore Dr. Travel for 1.4 miles, then turn left onto McFarlane Rd., right next to Peacock Park, where you should be able to find parking. If that lot happens to be full, try Kennedy Park, back north a short distance, on the east side of S. Bayshore Dr.

Mileage log

0.0	Turn right onto S. Bayshore Dr. Depending on the traffic, you may want to use the sidewalk or bike path.
1.4	Just after passing Vizcaya on your right, turn right at the traffic light onto 32nd Rd.
1.5	Turn left onto Brickell Ave.
1.9	Go through the gate at the end of the road and turn right. You are now on Rickenbacker Cswy.
2.0	Stay on the sidewalk/bike path and you won't have to bother with the tollbooth.
3.2	You have made it to the top of the bridge. Enjoy the view and the ride down the other side.
4.8	On your right is the Miami Seaquarium.
5.2	Cross another bridge.
7.8	Enter the village of Key Biscayne.
8.0	At the traffic light, turn right onto Harbor Dr.
9.4	Turn left at the roundabout onto W. Mashta Dr.
10.9	Turn left onto Crandon Blvd. at the traffic light and you are on your way back. (A right turn here will take you 0.4 mile to the Bill Baggs Cape Florida State Recreation Area where, after you pay a small entry fee, you will find beach access, places to swim and picnic, and a lighthouse to visit.)
16.4	You will want to cross over to the bike path on the south side of the road before you get to the bridge up ahead.
16.5	Cross the small bridge.
18.5	Cross the big bridge again.

19.7	Go past the tollbooth.
19.8	Turn left at the gate and you are back on Brickell Ave.
20.2	Turn right onto 32nd Rd.
20.3	At the traffic light, turn left onto S. Bayshore Dr.
21.7	Turn left onto McFarlane Rd., and you are done.

For more information, contact:
David Henderson, Coordinator
Metro-Dade Bicycle/Pedestrian Program
111 NW First St., Suite 910
Miami, FL 33128
(303) 375-1735

SHARK VALLEY LOOP

Location: Everglades National Park
Distance: 15 miles
Terrain: flat
Description: Although alligators are a common sight in Florida, it is rare to get an opportunity to cycle within jaw-snapping and tail-whipping reach of them. In fact, on the paved tram road at Shark

Please don't feed the gators. (Shark Valley in Everglades National Park)

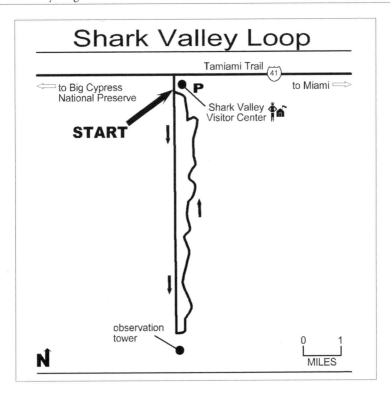

Shark Valley Loop

Tamiami Trail 41

to Big Cypress
National Preserve

P

to Miami

Shark Valley
Visitor Center

START

observation
tower

N

0   1
MILES

Valley it is sometimes necessary to swerve in order to avoid running over a 'gator that is sunning itself stretched out across the roadway. Do not let the thought of this frighten you off from this ride. These beasts are way more wary of you than you are of them. They eat things like fish, birds, and turtles. They do not eat people, and they also do not go out of their way to maliciously attack people. If you give them the measure of respect they (and all living things) deserve, you will get the satisfaction and unique honor of riding among them and other creatures of the Everglades. Snakes, crayfish, turtles, anhingas, herons, ibis, and various other fowl are commonly seen here. The best times to visit are early mornings and in the cooler months. Summer afternoons can be brutally hot, and there is little animal activity then anyway. No matter when you go, wear comfortable clothing and bring plenty of water and your sunscreen, because there is no shade to be found on this ride.

Fees: <$ 10 per-car entry fee

Facilities: Water, rest rooms, a telephone, drinks, snacks, tram tours, and bicycle rentals are all available here.

Finding the ride: From Miami, take the Tamiami Trail (US 41) north for about 30 miles, then turn left at the SHARK VALLEY entrance sign. From Naples, take the Tamiami Trail (US 41) south for about 70 miles, then turn right at the SHARK VALLEY entrance sign. The ride begins at the concession area.

Mileage log

0.0	Head south on the paved tram road leading away from the concession area. (Cyclists must ride the loop counter-clockwise.)
7.0	Park your bike in the rack and walk up the sidewalk to the observation tower—it's worth it. There are rest rooms here, too. When you are done, continue around the loop.
14.8	You have completed the loop and are back at the parking area.

For more information, contact:
Everglades National Park
40001 SR9336
Homestead, FL 33034-6733
(305) 242-7700
or
Shark Valley Tram Tours
(305) 221-8455
Website: www.sharkvalleytramtours.com

OFF-ROAD RIDES

OKEEHEELEE SOUTH PARK

Location: W. Palm Beach
Distance: 4 miles
Terrain: flat, moderately challenging single-track
Description: This new riding area is a welcome addition to the southeast Florida off-road cycling scene. It is not very big, and there are no fancy facilities, but it does offer what most area riders want

A melaleuca stand at Okeeheelee South Park

more than anything else: a place to ride their bikes. The Okeeheelee recreation area is managed by the Palm Beach County Parks and Recreation Department, who have kindly designated a small portion for off-road bicycling (the rest is for horseback riding). The trail is mostly single-track that winds through palmettos, Australian pines, and shady stands of melaleuca. There are several points on the trail where riders are offered two options. The "A" trails are for those with advanced riding skills. They typically take you up some tall dirt mound or over a steep drop-off. The "Bs" are for beginners, and they avoid those sorts of things by detouring you around them. As far as navigation goes, it does not matter which one you choose, because the trails always meet back up after the detour.

Fees: none

Facilities: There are no facilities at the trailhead.

Finding the ride: From I-95's exit 66, head west on Forest Hill Blvd. After about 6 miles, turn left into the entrance to Okeeheelee South Park (watch closely, it's not marked very well) just before crossing the bridge over the Florida Turnpike. Turn left into the dirt parking lot and park near the brown mountain-bike trail sign.

Mileage log

0.0   Enter the single-track behind the brown mountain bike trail sign. Follow the blue arrows. Stay to the left at the fork.

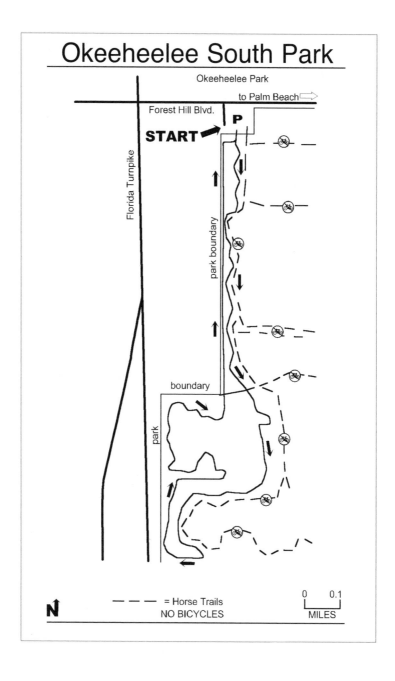

Okeeheelee South Park

Okeeheelee Park

to Palm Beach ⟹

Forest Hill Blvd.

P

START

Florida Turnpike

park boundary

boundary

park

N

– – – = Horse Trails
NO BICYCLES

0   0.1
MILES

0.2	The trail dips out near a double-track on the left, then dives right back into the woods.
0.9	Go straight across the dirt road, onto the gravel road.
1.0	Turn left onto the single-track.
1.3	Turn left onto the dirt road. Go straight across the next intersection, onto the single-track.
1.6	Stay to the left at the fork.
1.7	The trail makes a right turn and heads west.
2.1	The trail turns right and goes north along the turnpike.
2.3	Turn right onto the double-track.
2.5	Turn left onto the single-track, just past the left curve in the double-track.
3.0	You are back out near the turnpike.
3.7	Cross the dirt road.
4.4	You are back at the trailhead.

For more information, contact:
Palm Beach County Parks and Recreation Department
2700 6th Ave. S.
Lake Worth, FL 33461-4799
(561) 966-6600

DYER PARK

Location: West Palm Beach
Distance: 3 miles
Terrain: moderate single-track
Description: This crushed-shell and limestone gravel trail winds up, down, and around a 70-foot hill that is made mostly of garbage. That's right. Dyer Park is built on the site of an old landfill. It does sound kind of odd at first, but it is actually a good use for what would otherwise be a waste (no pun intended) of open space, a valuable commodity in south Florida. The trail itself is not the most interesting piece of single-track ever cut, and there is nary a patch of shade to be found on it. It does, however, offer south Floridians a place to try out their small chainrings, learn to ride switchbacks, and get a rare taste of

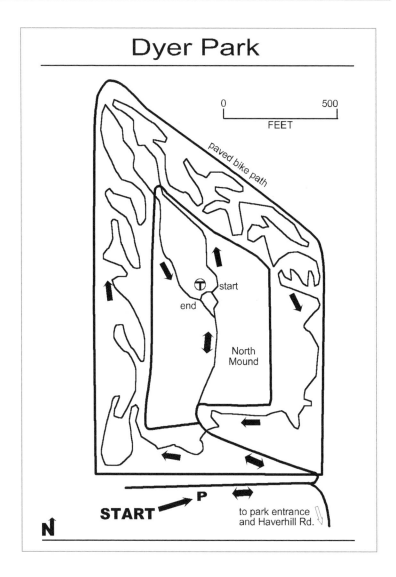

some gravity-induced speed. Aside from just offering a nice change of pace from the flat terrain found on the rest of the trails in the area. Dyer Park is a good place for a flatlander to prepare for a ride or race in hillier country.

Fees: none

Facilities: There are rest rooms, water, playgrounds, a paved bike path, and more at Dyer Park.

Finding the ride: From I-95's exit 74, take 45th St. west for 1.6

miles. Turn right onto Haverhill Rd. After 1.9 miles, turn left at the entrance to Dyer Park. Follow the main park road past the softball diamond and baseball fields for 0.9 mile. Park near the rest rooms at the soccer fields, on the left.

Mileage log

0.0	From the parking area near the soccer fields, turn right on the paved bike path, just across the drive for the parking area.
0.1	Take a sharp left at the large sign for the mountain bike trail and go up the hill.
0.2	Go straight onto the gravel road where the paved path makes a sharp right turn.
0.3	You are now at the top of the heap. Take a moment to catch your breath, enjoy the view, and ponder the colossal amount of rubbish it took to make this one of the highest points in south Florida. Then take the right-hand branch of the single-track in front of you.
0.5	Go straight across the paved bike path.
1.8	Cross the paved bike path again.
3.0	Turn right and go back up to the top of the hill.
3.1	Follow the gravel road back down to the paved bike path.
3.3	Make a sharp right turn at the bottom of the hill.
3.4	You are back at the parking area.

For more information, contact:
Palm Beach County Parks and Recreation Department
2700 6th Ave. S.
Lake Worth, FL 33461-4799
(561) 966-6600

MARKHAM PARK

Location: Sunrise
Distance: 5 miles
Terrain: easy to moderate double- and single-track
Description: The well-used trail system at Markham Park consists of 10 miles of single- and double-track trails. This popular park serves the needs of many recreational cyclists and is also used

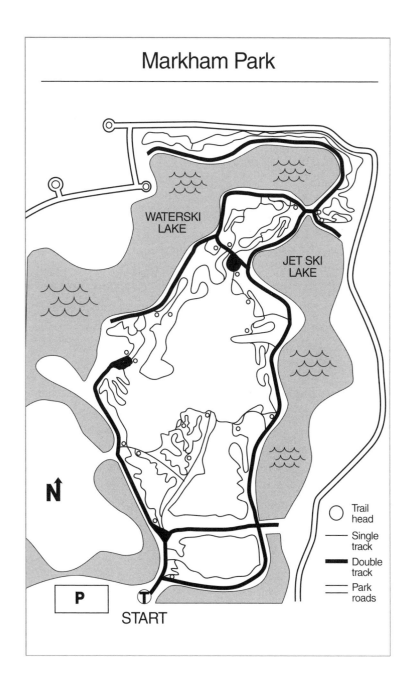

Markham Park

WATERSKI
LAKE

JET SKI
LAKE

N

Trail
head

Single
track

Double
track

Park
roads

P

START

as a racecourse from time to time. So it is no wonder that the trails are well established and easy to follow. They are marked with either green, signifying beginner level, or blue, indicating intermediate-level trails. There are some tricky parts and a few dirt mounds to climb and descend on the intermediate trails, but there are not too many sandy spots on any of the trails. The combination of very easy and moderately challenging terrain, plus the fact that it is not far from Pompano Beach, Ft. Lauderdale, or Hollywood, makes Markham Park a great place for most southwest Floridians to get down and dirty.

Fees: $1 entry fee on weekends and holidays, free during the week

Facilities: There are rest rooms, water, a snack bar, picnic areas, a swimming pool, a target shooting range, camping, and boat rentals available in the park.

Finding the ride: From Ft. Lauderdale, take I-595 west to exit 1A. From there, take SR 84 west for 2 miles, then turn right into the Markham Park entrance. After passing the gatehouse, go straight at the four-way stop. Take the third left, into the parking lot near the mountain-bike trailhead. Ride your bike over to the trailhead sign you passed on your way into the parking lot. Go through the gate and you are on the trail.

Mileage log: Because of the complexity of this trail network, no specific instructions are included here. As with other trails that see a lot of use (and sometimes abuse), riders have carved so many different little cutoffs and side trails that it is impractical to document them all. Riders are advised to consult the map in this book or pick up a copy of the trail map provided by the park. Most importantly, riders are encouraged to stay on the existing trails and out of the bike-restricted areas.

For more information, contact:
Markham Park
16001W.SR84
Sunrise, FL 33326
(954) 389-2000

OLETA RIVER STATE PARK

Location: N. Miami Beach
Distance: 7 miles
Terrain: ranges from easy to difficult single-track
Description: Oleta River State Park is the premier off-road riding location in southeast Florida. Its trails offer the best combination of qualities: They are well-maintained, as well as scenic and diverse, plus there is even some shade in places. Riders of all abilities can be entertained and challenged by the trails there. There is everything from wide, flat gravel roads to twisty, technical single-track, and even a few big dirt mounds to climb up and roll down. The trails are fairly well-marked as to their difficulty—beginner or intermediate—and are easy to follow. The directions below will show you how to link the various trail sections together in an efficient manner.

Fees: <$5 per vehicle park entry fee

Facilities: There are rest rooms, water, and a paved bike path at the park. The park visitor service also provides bike rentals.

Finding the ride: From the I-95/Florida Turnpike interchange in N. Miami, take N. Miami Beach Blvd. (SR 826 or NE 163rd St.) east for 5 miles and turn right into the park entrance. The gatehouse is 0.5 mile farther. Turn left into the parking area 0.7 mile past the gatehouse.

The single-track at Oleta River State Park, southeast Florida's finest

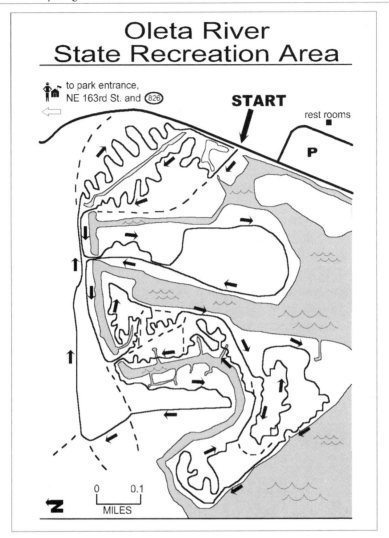

Oleta River State Recreation Area

to park entrance,
NE 163rd St. and (826)

START

rest rooms

P

0   0.1

MILES

To get to the trailhead, ride the paved bike path back along the park drive you came in on. The trailhead will be on your left after about 0.1 mile.

Mileage log

0.0   Enter the trail at the trailhead kiosk. It starts out as a dirt road.

0.1   Turn right onto the intermediate single-track.

0.6   Turn right onto the dirt road and then turn left at the intersection.

0.7	Turn left at the next dirt road, then immediately left again onto the intermediate single track.
0.9	Turn left onto the dirt road, then left at the fork.
1.4	Go straight at the fork.
1.5	Turn left at the intersection.
1.7	Turn left onto the dirt road, then left again onto the intermediate single-track.
2.2	Turn right onto the dirt road.
2.4	Turn left onto the dirt road, then immediately left onto the intermediate single-track.
2.8	Turn right onto the dirt road.
2.9	The road narrows down to a single-track here.
3.1	Go straight where the novice trail turns right.
3.8	Turn left onto the dirt road, then left again onto the intermediate single-track.
4.1	Go straight across the dirt road and cross the bridge.
4.3	Turn left onto the dirt road and left again onto the intermediate single-track.
4.9	Turn right onto the dirt road.
5.0	Go straight at the intersection.
5.1	Turn right at the intersection.
5.4	Turn right, then left, at the camping cabins.
5.5	Turn right onto the last (and toughest) section of the intermediate single-track.
6.5	You are back at the trailhead.

For more information, contact:
Oleta River State Park
3400 NE 163rd St.
N. Miami Beach, FL 33160
(305) 919-1946

LONG PINE KEY NATURE TRAIL

Location: Everglades National Park
Distance: 13 miles
Terrain: flat, easy double-track

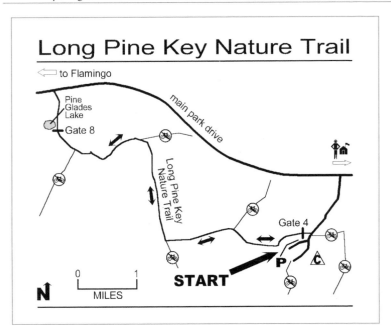

Description: This 13-mile out-and-back starts at the Long Pine Key Campground and Picnic Area and terminates at Pine Glades Lake. In between, the limestone road mainly travels grassy pinelands with a bit of sawgrass prairie thrown in for good measure. There is some, but not a lot, of shade along the way. The riding is easy and the scenery is great on this hard, flat surface. There may be some flooding, and there most definitely will be lots of biting insects in the summer months. The best time to do this one is November through February.

Fees: <$15 entry fee per vehicle to enter Everglades National Park. Plan to spend the day—there is plenty to see and do.

Facilities: There are rest rooms and water at the picnic area. There is also a campground adjacent to the picnic area.

Finding the ride: From Miami, take either US 1, the Florida Turnpike, or Krome Ave. (SR 997) to Florida City. From Florida City go west on SR 9336 (SW 344th St./W. Palm Dr.) for 1.5 miles. Turn left onto Tower Rd. (SW 192nd Ave.) at the four-way stop. After 2.1 miles, turn right at the four-way stop sign onto Ingraham Hwy. (SW 376th St.). Continue for 6.3 miles to the park entrance station. From there, take the main park drive 4 miles and turn left at the LONG PINE KEY CAMPGROUND AND PICNIC AREA sign. Go 1.4 miles and park in the lot near the rest rooms.

Mileage log

0.0	Starting from the parking area near the rest rooms at Long Pine Key Picnic Area, ride back up the road you came in on for 0.2 mile.
0.2	Turn left onto the gravel road, go through Gate 4, and you are on the nature trail.
1.6	Stay to the left here, where the hiking-only trail branches off to the right.
2.8	Turn right here, where another hiking-only trail comes in from the left.
4.4	Stay to the left here, where yet another hiking-only trail branches off to the right.
5.8	Go straight past the hiking trail on your left.
6.3	Go through Gate 8 and have a look at Pine Glades Lake, on the left side of the road. This is the turnaround point and a nice place for a rest. When you are done here, go back through the gate and back the way you came.
6.8	Go straight past the hiking trail on your right.
8.2	Stay to the right.
9.8	Turn left.
11.0	Stay to the right.
12.4	Go through Gate 4 and turn right onto the paved road.
12.6	You are back at the picnic area.

For more information, contact:
Everglades National Park
40001 SR 9336
Homestead, FL 33034-6733
(305) 242-7700

OTHER RIDES IN SOUTHEAST FLORIDA

ROAD

The Florida Keys Bike Tour is a two-day, 101-mile loop from the Chekika ranger station in Everglades National Park, southwest of Miami, to John Pennekamp Coral Reef State Park, in Key Largo. This trip is designed to take a full weekend, with camping at John

Pennekamp, but some mileage hogs like to make it a day trip. Free maps and directions are available from the Florida Department of Environmental Protection.

Contact:

Florida Department of Environmental Protection.

Office of Greenways and Trails

Mail Station 795

3900 Commonwealth Blvd.

Tallahassee, FL 32399-3000

(850) 487-4784

Old Cutler Road has a bike path that begins just south of Coconut Grove and extends 15 miles southward. It passes Matheson Hammock Park, the Charles Deering Estate Historic Site, and Biscayne National Park. Metered parking is available at Coconut Grove, and parking is also available at Matheson Hammock Park.

Contact:

Miami-Dade Parks and Recreation

(305) 755-7800

Lake Okeechobee Scenic Trail (LOST) is a paved and off-road trail that winds around Lake Okeechobee, atop the Herbert Hoover Dike, and also through nearby communities such as Clewiston and Belle Glade. Plans are in the works for a paved 120-mile trail running atop the Lake Okeechobee dike system through six counties, connecting numerous parks and recreation areas.

Contact:

Florida Greenways and Trails

(863) 983-8101 Monday- Friday

(772) 219-4575 weekends

OFF ROAD

DuPuis Reserve State Forest, located just east of Lake Okeechobee, offers almost 20 miles of biking on forest roads. While there are many additional miles of trails, these are not open to bicycles. The forest is often closed on fall and winter weekends for hunting and is located west of Indiantown, on FL 76.

Contact:
DuPuis Reserve State Forest
HCR 1144
Canal Point, FL 33438
(407) 924-8021

Jonathan Dickinson State Park offers both paved and off-road riding. There is a paved 1.5-mile path and more than 13 miles of looping double-track. In addition, hiking is allowed on the horse trails in the park. Maps can be picked up at the entrance station, where entry fees are collected.

Contact:
Jonathan Dickinson State Park
16450 SE Federal Hwy.
Hobe Sound, FL 33455
(722) 546-2771

Old Ingram Highway, located in Everglades National Park, is a 20-mile out-and-back dirt service road that leads into one of the less visited areas of the park. This area is known for its healthy population of deer flies in summer, so be ready to outride them. The ride is located off the main park road near the Royal Palm Visitor Center. The park charges an entry fee.

Contact:
Everglades National Park
40001 SR 9336
Homestead, FL 33034-6733
(305) 242-7700

Broward County Parks
There are several parks in Broward County that have short, paved bicycle trails suitable for family outings and easy rides. These parks also offer many other recreation opportunities. They are generally open during the day and closed at night; call ahead for specific hours. Entry is usually free during the week, but there is a small fee on weekends and holidays.

Contact:
Tradewinds Park
3600 W. Sample Rd.

Coconut Creek, FL 33073
(954) 968-3880
Website: www.broward.org/parks/tw.htm

T. Y. Park
3300 N. Park Rd.
Hollywood, FL 33021
(954) 985-1980

C. B. Smith Park
900 N. Flamingo Rd.
Pembroke Pines, FL 33028
(954) 437-2650
Website: www.broward.org/parks/cb.htm

BICYCLE CLUBS OF SOUTHEAST FLORIDA

Boca Raton Bicycle Club
P.O Box 810744
Boca Raton, FL 33481-0744
Hotline: (561) 391- 6109
Website: bocaratonbicycleclub.com

Miami Masters
Contact: Fernando Angel
(305) 222-0157
Website: http://prpa-upc.com/miamimasters/miamimasters.htm
E-mail: team@miamimasters.com
Interests: road racing

South Broward Wheelers Bicycle Club
P.O. Box 290723
Davie. FL 33329
Contact: Richard L. Berger, D.D.S., Treasurer
E-mail: treasurer@southbrowardwheelers.com
Website: www.southbrowardwheelers.com
Interests: road, time trials, some touring
Annual events: annual century, early September; Christmas ride

for Toys for Tots charity, December; large monthly rides from Brian
Piccolo Park

Everglades Bicycle Club
P.O. Box 430282
South Miami, FL 33243
Website: http://evergladesbc.com
E-mail: info@evergladesbc.com

Treasure Coast Cycling Association
P.O. Box 2559
Stuart, FL 34995-2559
Website: http://treasurecoastcycling.netfirms.com
E-mail: tccainfo@adelphia.net

Appendices

STATE AND NATIONAL CONTACTS
Contact the following for free information on public lands in Florida:
Florida Department of Environmental Protection
Office of Greenways and Trails
3900 Commonwealth Blvd.
Mail Station 795
Tallahassee, FL 32399-3000
(850) 245-2052 or (800) 822-5208
Website: http://www.dep.state.fl.us/gwt

Florida Division of Forestry
Department of Agriculture and Consumer Services
2005 Apalachee Pkwy.
Tallahassee, FL 32301
(850) 922-2966

State Bicycle/Pedestrian Coordinator
605 Suwannee St.
Mail Station 82
Tallahassee, FL 32399-0450
(850) 414-4100

Northwest Florida Water Management District
81 Water Management Dr.
Havana, FL 32333-4712

(850) 539-5999
Website: www.nwfwmd.state.fl.us

St. Johns River Water Management District
P.O. Box 1429
Palatka, FL 32178-1429
(386) 329-500 or (800) 451-7106

South Florida Water Management District
3301 Gun Club Rd.
W. Palm Beach, FL 33406
(407) 686-8800

Southwest Florida Water Management District
2379 Broad St. (US 41 S.)
Brooksville, FL 34609-6899
(352) 796-7211 or (800) 423-1476
Website: www.swfwmd.state.fl.us

Suwannee River Water Management District
9225 CR 49
Live Oak, FL 32060
(386) 362-1001 or(800)226-1066
Website: www.srwmd.state.fl.us

STATE BICYCLE ORGANIZATIONS
Bike Florida, Inc.
P.O Box 5295
Gainesville, FL 32627
(352) 392-8093
Website: www.bikeflorida.org
E-mail: info@bikeflorida.org
Bike Florida is a yearly recreational coast-to-coast ride across Florida,
offering both three- and six-day options.

Florida Bicycle Association (FBA)
P.O Box 718
Waldo, FL 32694

Contact: Henry Lawrence
Website: http://www.flbicycle.org/
E-mail: hnlbicycle@yahoo.com

NATIONAL BICYCLE ORGANIZATIONS
National Off-Road Bicycle Association (NORBA)
USA Cycling, Inc.
1 Olympic Plaza
Colorado Springs, CO 80909
(719) 866-4581; fax: (719) 866-4628
Website: http://www.usacycling.org
E-mail: membership@usacycling.org

International Mountain Bicycling Association (IMBA)
P.O. Box 7578
Boulder, CO 80306
Street address:
5541 Central Ave., #201
Boulder, CO 80301
(303) 545-9011; fax: (303) 545-9026
Website: http://www.imba.com/
E-mail: info@imba.com

U.S. Cycling Federation (USCF)
1 Olympic Plaza
Colorado Springs, CO 80909
(719) 866-4581
Website: http://www.usacycling.org
E-mail: membership@usacycling.org

League of American Bicyclists (LAB)
1612KS1 NW, Suite 800
Washington, DC 20006-2850
(202) 822-1333; fax: (202) 822-1334
Website: http://www.bikeleague.org/
E-mail: bikeleague@bikeleague.org

ADDITIONAL RESOURCES

Florida State Park Guide
Division of Recreation and Parks
Department of Environmental Protection
3900 Commonwealth Blvd.
Mail Station 535
Tallahassee, FL 32399-3000
(850) 245-2157
Website: http://www.dep.state.fl.us/parks/

National Forests in Florida: Recreation Area Directory
USDA Forest Service
Woodcrest Office Park
325 John Knox Rd., Suite F-100
Tallahassee, FL 32303
(850) 523-8500
Website: www.fs.fed.us/r8/florida

Florida Bicycle Trails
www.visitflorida.com
or the cycling section of the following website:
www.visitflorida.com/landing.php/experience/nature/cycling

Rails to Trails Conservancy
www.railtrails.org

Florida State Parks
www.floridastateparks.org

Florida State Forests
www.fl-dof.com

Glossary

big ring: the large chainring on a bicycle, used when riding at a fast pace

century: a 100-mile ride

chainring: one of the front cogs on a bicycle

chamois: the padding in the crotch of cycling shorts

criterium: a mass-start race consisting of many laps around a short course (usually less than 1 mile), often with tight, tricky corners and turns

cyclocross bike: a lightweight bicycle made for a combination of on- and off-road riding, usually equipped with drop (10 speed–style) handlebars and knobby tires of moderate width

double-track: an unpaved path or road, wide enough for the passage of a car, truck, or jeep

gatorback: the above-ground root of the palmetto

hybrid: a multipurpose bicycle suitable for both casual pavement riding and easy off-road riding, usually equipped with flat or upright handlebars and tires of moderate width

little ring: the smallest chainring on a bicycle, used when climbing steep hills or just taking it easy

metric century: a 100-kilometer (62-mile) ride

middle ring: the middle chainring on a bicycle, used when riding at a moderate pace or on mild hills

mountain bike: a bicycle made for rugged off-road riding, usually equipped with flat handlebars and wide, knobby tires

rail-trail: a recreational trail built on an old railroad corridor

road bike: a lightweight bicycle made for high-speed pavement riding, usually equipped with drop (10 speed–style) handlebars and narrow, high-pressure tires

single-track: a narrow, unpaved trail wide enough for the passage of only one cyclist or hiker at a time

tandem: a bicycle built for two

technical: requiring a high degree of skill and technique

time trial: a staggered-start race in which cyclists ride alone and compete for the fastest time over a given course

track bike: a bicycle made for racing at a velodrome

velodrome: a banked oval track made for bicycle racing

Here are some other books from Pineapple Press on related topics. For a complete catalog, write to Pineapple Press, P.O. Box 3889, Sarasota, Florida 34230-3889, or call (800) 746-3275. Or visit our website at www.pineapplepress.com.

Easygoing Guide to Natural Florida, Volume 1: South Florida by Douglas Waitley. If you love nature but want to enjoy it with minimum effort, this is the book for you. This is the first of three volumes that will cover the entire state. (pb)

Fishing Adventures in Florida by Max D. Hunn. Join the author as he steers through the twisted mangrove channels of the Ten Thousand Islands, dodging "noggin-knockers" and oyster bars on the outgoing tide, searching for the "big one." (pb)

Florida's Finest Inns and Bed & Breakfasts by Bruce Hunt. Guide to 135 wonderful Florida accommodations, from the Panhandle to Key West. (pb)

Running in Florida by Mauricio Herreros. Information on the top 150 places to run in Florida and the 150 best races in Florida. Gives complete direction and mileage of each run, plus extended variations. Includes names and addresses of running clubs, general references, and a pace chart. (pb)

Sea Kayaking in Florida, 2nd Edition by David and Mark Gluckman. Fully revised guide to a fast-growing water sport for both novices and experienced kayakers. Includes information on gear, maps, campsite guides, and more. (pb)

Visiting Small-Town Florida, Revised Edition by Bruce Hunt. Guide to 70 of Florida's most charming, historic, and often eclectic small towns—places with names like Sopchoppy, Ozello, and Two Egg. Includes directions and contact information. (pb)